MANAGING *your* MONKEY

MIND FITNESS

CHANGE YOUR LIFE • SAVE YOUR LIFE

"Stress is like gasoline on the fire of aging."
Dr. Kara Fitzgerald,
author of *Younger You*

• • • •

"My brain is like a hamster on a wheel, and it won't come off. I've been dealing with it all my life."
Reese Witherspoon,
Academy Award winning actress and
successful businesswoman

• • • •

"Baseball is 90% mental, and the other half is physical"
Yogi Berra

• • • •

"External circumstances cannot create lasting happiness -- the right state of mind can"
Dalai Lama

ENDORSEMENTS

Joe Bailey
*Former COO National Football League World League,
CEO Miami Dolphins*

"Everyone needs a framework, and nothing more important today than a framework or a roadmap on how to achieve mental balance and equilibrium in our lives. I spent a good part of my career running large professional sports teams and leagues. In chapter four you will read about the anxiety and stress faced by professional athletes and other performers. Physical skills and conditioning have always been key. Mind fitness is a more recent focus for most of these teams, their coaches and players. Most are paid very well, but, face mental challenges both on the field and off that we can only imagine. I have witnessed this up close, and want to highly recommend this book and the Six Pillars regimen outlined here. Alan has given us a framework for areas that are vital and key to achieving balance. It is up to us to adopt it."

• • • •

Dr Melanie Greenberg
Author of Best-Selling book, The Stress-Proof Brain

"My professional life is spent with clients who are struggling with all the stressors of life today. The stress and anxiety, at record levels before Covid are orders of magnitude greater now. For most, the resilience required to navigate the choppy seas of mental health and mind fitness don't come without a regimen of practices proven to provide such health and fitness. In my best-selling book, The Stress-Proof Brain, I provided a recommended set of practices, including many of those Alan includes in the Six Pillars Regimen that you will find in this book. Mind fitness doesn't require all the artificial substances being used by so many. I highly recommend this book to you and encourage you to explore how these practices can help you in your own life."

Author of Best-Selling book, The Stress-Proof Brain and practicing psychologist, author, speaker, life/business coach. A popular media expert, she has been featured on numerous major media networks and publications.

• • • •

Mike Critelli
Retired CEO Pitney Bowes, current Co-Founder and CEO MakeUsWell.

"Alan masterfully links three broad societal issues: the insecurities we carry from childhood, the unique issues women confront in managing their insecurities, and how social media has distorted and amplified these problems. His optimistic message is that while all of us struggle with these issues, we can individually gain control over them. This is a uniquely personal and powerful commentary."

• • • •

Jacqueline Hayes
a four-time author, keynote speaker, impact coach, publisher and entrepreneur.

I have always been highly motivated and driven by the desire to achieve my dreams and goals, to the point of putting my work and my success before my health and my wellbeing. Result-- an advanced state of burnout. In pain and deeply tormented inside, my doctors, unable to find the cause were willing to prescribe medications. Frustrated and exhausted, I realized that I had to take responsibility for my health and wellbeing. My lifestyle and priorities were totally out of order. I have adopted new habits that have transformed my life. I now put myself first. I enjoy daily practices such as prayer, meditation, yoga, a plant-based diet, gratitude and reading great books. You can take control of your mind and your life. I highly recommend this book and the suggested Six Pillars to you for your own life.

Honorable Andrew Card
White House Chief of Staff, former Secretary of Transportation,
Dean of Bush School of Government at Texas A&M University

"We are in the midst of an unprecedented mental health crisis. Coping with the pace and stress of life today is a challenge for all of us. The impact of the Covid pandemic along with the toxicity of our politics today has created an environment that too many can't deal with, without self-medicating with substances that are health-destroying and in too many cases fatal. Kathleene and I already practice several of the Six Pillars. There is a way to manage the stress and anxiety of this unprecedented period in our country's history. You can find your own regimen here and I highly recommend it to you."

· · · ·

Flavio Ungaro
Chief Executive, Mentally Fit Institute, Latin America,
former Professional Player and Coach

"For the professional athlete, the monkey gets very loud during critical moments in a game. The pressures of social media and all the commentary on your performance are often more difficult to manage than the physical demands of the sport. The theme of this book is mind fitness and how to manage the game between the ears. Having experienced this first-hand during my career, and recognizing that the same mind management lessons apply to business and the professions, I am now in the business of preparing management teams and others for the hyper-competitive business landscape of today. I highly recommend the Six Pillars to you for your personal life. This book provides you the roadmap."

· · · ·

Colonel June Copeland

Director of Business Systems Architecture, Department of Army, West Point graduate Veteran of Operation Iraqi Freedom, and Operation Spartan Shield

"Discipline and devotion to duty is the foundation of any effective military force. Cadets graduating from West Point have these principles deeply ingrained into our character. I have commanded in the field and served at the Pentagon in multiple force-wide initiatives. The stress level is high for everyone. Serving in these roles is an order of magnitude higher for a woman in an institution that has been male-centric for most of human history. My experience has shown me it is even more so for a woman of color walking the tight-rope of not being perceived as "a black woman with attitude." Managing the stress of service during wartime; raising three daughters (all West Pointers themselves) while maintaining my health have been some of my greatest challenges. I recently had a stress related health setback. We are blessed with these magnificent bodies and no maintenance manual. I am blessed to have recently discovered and incorporated many of the Six Pillars that Alan recommends in this book. These pillars have given me new insights and have been a tremendous help to me! I highly recommend it to each of the readers."

• • • •

Dr Kara Fitzgerald

ND, IFMCP, Author of groundbreaking book Younger You, A leading voice in the intersection of nutrition, epigenetics, and aging, Dr. Fitzgerald's work has been featured in media outlets such as Prevention, Fast Company, MSN, Everyday Health for Functional Medicine

"All of us recognize stress and anxiety and its symptoms. Especially today, it is our constant companion. Well reported are the coping mechanisms many use to self-medicate with health destroying substances like opioids, alcohol, binge eating, etc. Little recognized until recently is the dramatic affect unmanaged and undigested stress has on our aging process. Our chronological age is often more and in some cases can be much less than our birthday suggests. As I state in my new book, Younger You, 'Stress is gasoline on the fire of aging', and you can become younger than you are today" In this book, Alan lays out a regimen that if practiced consistently will help you not only live longer but with more vitality and vibrancy."

. . . .

Colonel Jamie Alden

Retired Special Forces Lieutenant Colonel, Jamie Alden, West Point graduate, served 4 combat tours over a ten-year period in Afghanistan

"The fog of war is often written about. It is experienced first-hand by those who are deployed to far away battlefields. After West Point, I was deployed four times over a ten-year period to Afghanistan. A commanding general once said that no battle plan lasts beyond the first shots being fired. Keep moving, shooting and adapting until the smoke clears, he said. Managing a racing, anxious mind in the midst of an engagement that could take your life is a challenge unlike most any of us will experience. The Special Forces and other branches are adopting mindfulness and other similar techniques to those in the Six Pillars regimen outlined by Alan in this book. Susan and I, both West Point graduates, have for years practiced these techniques and we both highly recommend them to you."

. . . .

Steve Chapman
Syndicated columnist and for mer member of Chicago Tribune Editorial Board

"Anyone who follows the news these days may be tempted to follow journalist Michael Kinsley's recommendation: "Please don't remain calm." Anxiety, fear, anger and despair all seem like reasonable responses to the scary world we live in. But succumbing to the chronic churn of negative emotions – ceding control to the "monkey mind" – is no way to help your country, your community or yourself. Alan Steelman, a wise man who has known both success and failure in politics and business, offers a concise, practical plan for achieving the mental equilibrium needed to navigate our turbulent times. I think you'll find it more than worth your while."

• • • •

ABOUT THE AUTHOR

Alan is a best-selling author, a former member of the U.S. Congress, a former member of the White House staff, and former vice-chairman of Alexander Proudfoot Company. He has been a chairman of the Dallas Council on World Affairs and a board member of Sterling Software (NYSE), Aristocrat Technologies (ASX), and the Texas Growth Fund. He is a graduate of Baylor University and holds a master's degree from SMU He also was a resident fellow at the Institute of Politics at Harvard University. He is a certified yoga instructor.

His career in politics was marked with distinction. *Time Magazine* featured him as one of the 200 Emerging Young Leaders in the United States. *The Dallas Times Herald, on the other hand,* referred to him as "one of the best ever sent to Congress from Texas." Lastly, *New Times Magazine* named him one of the top ten best congressmen in the country during his second term.

A family history of manic depression on his father's side of the family inspires his writing on the topic of mental health. His only brother took his life at age 36 and his father and three of his five brothers also struggled with bi-polar depression.

CONTENTS

THE MONKEY

The Monkey Mind: "The Ides of March, famous as the day that Julius Caesar was assassinated, is noteworthy for me as it's the day I was born. On that day, God gave me breath… and a monkey. I'm thankful for the breath…not so much for the monkey." —Alan Steelman

The incessant mind chatter that is with us from an early age has been referred to as the "monkey mind." It is our inner critic—the voice of self-gaslighting. The products of all this ruminating and frenetic chatter are stress, anxiety, depression, and other debilitating mental conditions. Monkey management is the biggest influence on the four biggest factors in our lives: success (self-limiting beliefs), aging (epigenetics), physical health (undigested stress), and mental well-being (ability to surf the choppy seas of life). The monkey, when properly managed, provides the motivation to move forward with our goals in life. Left to roam freely the contours of our mind, it destroys peace of mind, creates disease (95% of chronic illness is lifestyle related and is modifiable with the changes outlined here), and prematurely ages us.

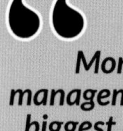

Monkey management is the biggest influence on the four biggest factors in our lives: success (self-limiting beliefs), aging (epigenetics), physical health (undigested stress), and mental well-being (ability to surf the choppy seas of life).

In his first inaugural address to the nation, as the Civil War was raging, Abraham Lincoln called upon the "better angels of our nature" to reunite the country and stop the bloodshed. We are body, mind, and spirit. The better angels dwell in the spirit -- where kindness, gratitude, generosity, and our finer qualities reside. All acts of violence are triggered by an agitated mind. Anger, jealousy, envy, wrath, lust, and the rest of the seven sins are products of thoughts and events that rise and agitate the mind. The monkey is the voice of the agitated mind. Dalai Lama has said that if we could teach every eight-year-old to meditate, we could heal the planet of violence in one generation. The monkey can be silenced or -- at the least -- become less of an influence on our thoughts and behavior by incorporating the Six Pillars regimen outlined in here.

In this book, you will find a full diagnosis of this and a detailed regimen to help you achieve a life of mental and physical equilibrium and peace of mind. These are keys to a happy and productive life. Plus, there is a whole chapter, backed by science, devoted to how you can actually get younger.

I have a love-hate relationship with mine. It's provided the drive and the low-level anxiety throughout my life for everything I've accomplished. Properly managed, the monkey gets you out of bed in the morning with the motivation to make your plan/work your plan. For me, It has also been that "nattering nabob" of worry, anxiety, and stress. It costs me sleep; it has caused me to "stress eat" and was responsible for a case of imposter syndrome during my political career and a case of validation-need -- fear of anonymity -- that persists to this day. The monkey is the ever-present companion to each of us. It is my hope that you will find your own way, from the methods and life examples you will find here, to at least get yours onto a leash that will allow you to rein him/her in as needed.

BECOMING *WELLTHY:* MIND FITNESS

"Obsession with the Emerald City and forgetting to enjoy the Yellow Brick Road"

In his book titled *Wellth,* Jason Wachob redefines successful living as one of abundance, happiness, purpose, health, and joy. This is opposed to the pursuit of what most of us spend our lives in pursuit of: a large amount of money and possessions, often to the exclusion of the other dimensions of our lives. Yes, financial security is important and is a big contributor to peace of mind. The challenge is in knowing how much is enough, and never to the exclusion of the other more important pillars.

The late Zig Ziglar, the famous and highly regarded motivational speaker, told the story of a very wealthy Canadian man who came to see him about his life and why he was so unhappy and miserable despite being wealthy beyond any dreams he had as a young man. Ziglar asked him how his relationship was with his children, wife, friends, physical health, etc. He answered that he was estranged from his children, on his fourth marriage, had no friends close enough to confide his struggles with, and was on blood-pressure medicine and pain medication -- wealthy, not wellthy.

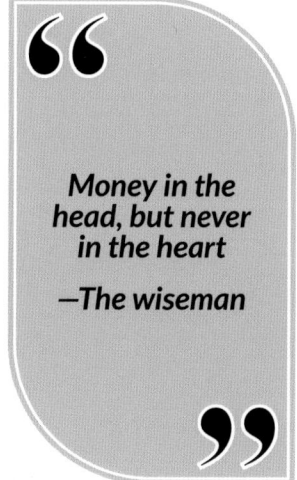

Money in the head, but never in the heart

—The wiseman

This is the story of so many lives today. Clay Cockrell, founder of *Walk and Talk Therapy*, is a psychiatrist and counselor to high-net worth individuals, including several billionaires. He says that trust issues, lack of a sense of purpose, and struggles with shame guilt and fear mark the lives of many of his clients.

Steve Job's Final Words for Us All

"I have come to the pinnacle of success in business.
In the eyes of others, my life has been the symbol of success.

However, apart from work, I have little joy.
Finally, my wealth is simply a fact to which I am accustomed.
At this time, lying on the hospital bed and remembering all my life, I realize that all the accolades and riches of which I was once so proud, have become insignificant, with my imminent death.
In the dark, when I look at green lights, of the equipment for artificial respiration and feel the buzz of their mechanical sounds, I can feel the breath of my approaching death looming over me.
Only now do I understand that once you accumulate enough money for the rest of your life, you must pursue objectives that are not related to wealth.

It should be something more important:
For example, stories of love, art, dreams of my childhood.
No, stop pursuing wealth, it can only make a person into a twisted being, just like me.
God has made us one way, we can feel the love in the heart of each of us, and not illusions built by fame or money, like I made in my life, I cannot take them with me.
I can only take with me the memories that were strengthened by love.
This is the true wealth that will follow you; will accompany you, he will give strength and light to go ahead.

Love can travel thousands of miles and so life has no limits. Move to where you want to go. Strive to reach the goals you want to achieve. Everything is in your heart and in your hands.
What is the world's most expensive bed? The hospital bed.
You, if you have money, you can hire someone to drive your car, but you cannot hire someone to take your illness that is killing you.
Material things lost can be found. But one thing you can never find once you have lost it, is life.
Whatever stage of life where we are right now, at the end we will have to face the day when the curtain falls.
Please treasure your family love, love for your spouse, love for your friends...

Treat everyone well and stay friendly with your neighbors."

For those who think that fame and fortune bring happiness and mental balance, the irony is that those who seem to "have it all" are often among the most troubled. The norm for most is that external circumstances like fame, money, and social position will bring happiness.

"My brain is like a hamster on a wheel, and it won't come off. I've been dealing with it all my life." (Reese Witherspoon, Academy Award winning actress and successful businesswoman)

By all outward appearances, she seems stable and successful, yet she struggles like so many with achieving inner peace.

LeAnn Rimes, another famous and successful entertainer, says, "I have struggled with anxiety and depression for much of my life. Amidst all the joy and success, I've had so much emptiness and sadness."

Examples of celebrities with mental challenges, so chronic and acute that they had a fatal end, are many: Elvis Presley, Marilyn Monroe, Kurt Cobain, Whitney Houston, Prince, Anthony Bourdain, Judy Garland, etc.

Why this book? We manage our spiritual lives through meditation, prayer and worship, and many follow physical fitness regimens to achieve body fitness. Yet, for most of us the biggest life challenge is managing our MIND FITNESS. The pace of life in the digital age has become too much for many without self-medicating with health and life-destroying substances. Job losses, business closings, social isolation, deaths of loved ones and more total loss of life than all U.S. wars combined, except for the Civil Ward from the Covid-19 pandemic, added a layer of stress on what was already a mental health epidemic.

Deaths from stress-related causes are at unprecedented levels. It has been called the Black Plague of Our Age. On top of 9-11-2001, which took national stress levels to an all-time high, comes CoVid-19 and the pace of life goes from too fast to a dead stop for most. The dead stop didn't last, but the stress and anxiety from the pace of life becomes fear and panic for some to the point of being uncertain about what the future holds. We remind ourselves that we will work through this, and we will; yet the changes to what was the norm are certain to affect all of the most important areas of our lives.

Anxiety, unmanaged, becomes chronic and, for many, debilitating. The amygdala, a small almond- shaped mass of gray matter in our brain manages our response to the events in our lives -- more on this in the chapter on the Mind and the Brain -- two different things. The amygdala is our fight or flight warning system, and is triggered by events that potentially pose threats to our well-being. But a normal amount is meant to help keep us safe, experts say.

"The emotion of anxiety and the underlying physiological stress response evolved to protect us," Wendy Suzuki, a neuroscientist and the author of *Good Anxiety*, says. Learning to manage stress is doable for most. Those with clinically diagnosed conditions should, of course, seek professional help.

My Story

There was a bipolar gene in my family on my father's side. He and three of his brothers had it and suffered from depression throughout their lives. My only sibling, my brother, Terry, inherited it and struggled with it from the age of 10 until he took his life at the age of 36 with a gunshot. By pure luck of the genetic lottery, I didn't inherit it. I have had event-related episodes of depression at certain intervals in my life. I lost a race for the U.S. Senate and was depressed and adrift for about a year afterward. I got fired as President of Alexander Proudfoot after leading a failed effort to oust the Chairman of the Board and have experienced a diagnosable condition called Seasonal Adaptive Depression (SAD) usually during February of each year and lasts for about three weeks. This is a condition that is pretty common among those who don't adapt to colder weather, rain, and snow.

None of us ever get out of high school

It has been more of our family circumstances while growing up that continues to feed my anxiety. There's a saying, "None of us ever get out of high school." Meaning, these developmental years and our experience during that time hardwire us in certain ways that influence our behavior and mindset for the remainder of our lives. Articles and books written by women in midlife or later appear fairly often of the proverbial "mean girl" syndrome and the bullying or verbal harassment they endured in high school.

I grew up in a family of unconditional love. I never heard a single word from either parent that made me feel less about myself. There were plenty of times, especially during my teen years, when my behavior certainly deserved critical commentary. I took this unconditional love for granted, assuming it was the norm. I learned much later about parental verbal abuse, if not physical abuse, from parents who were stressed and pressured from their own life conditions and took it out on their spouses and children.

My dad was a member of the Steelworkers Union and my mother a member of the Garment Workers Union. In addition to the stress my brother's condition was causing them, there was a recession and later a strike by the union. The combination meant we had my mother's income from her job as a seamstress and my dad's unemployment check. I had jobs from the seventh grade forward, including the local Dairy Queen, the downtown movie theatre, the drive-in theatre, hauling hay in the summertime, clearing right-of-way for Arkansas Power and Light, a paper route, picking and selling pecans, a radio disc jockey, and several others. All the above wired me to be vigilant always on future events that could jeopardize me and my family's well-being. Put simply, the monkey is always talking about regrets from the past or fears about the future. This book and the Six Pillars, outlined in chapter six, are tools that we can use to sedate the monkey and help us to "be here now." Having said that, I still all these years later keep one eye over my shoulder.

Fear of anonymity…gaining on me

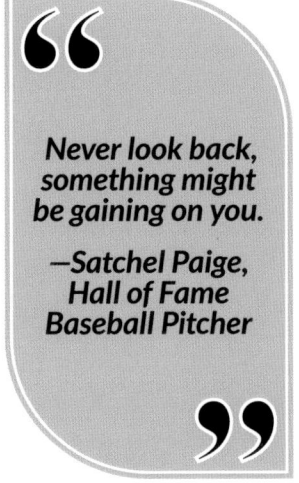

Never look back, something might be gaining on you.

—Satchel Paige, Hall of Fame Baseball Pitcher

With the benefit of time and hindsight, I have come to realize in recent years that a primary driver in my life has been a fear of not being seen, to matter, to be visible, the need for validation by others. Why would a sixth grader run for graduating class president and editor of the grade school paper at the same time, and the same pattern in college -- class president, student congress, and fraternity president. Seven years out of college at age 29, running for and getting elected to the U.S. Congress, then for the U. S. Senate (unsuccessfully) four years later. A best-selling book, *I'm Ok, You're Ok* was written in 1967 on the need we all have for approval and validation. Not too many have that need so deep-seated that they will go head-to-head in full view of everyone and endure all the rigors of political campaigns in order to have more voters choose you than the other person. To the candidate, it is an ultimate stamp of "you're ok."

An anecdote from high school illustrates the need for applause that I had. Although baseball was my favorite sport, I played the others, as well. I hated football, but played, nevertheless. Young boys, especially teenagers all need ways to prove their manhood, and football was seen as one of the ultimate tests. I played fullback and enjoyed hearing the public address announcer say things like, "Steelman off tackle for a four-yard gain and a first down." About halfway through the season, one of our linemen got injured and because I was one of the bigger players on the team, the coach assigns me to the line as a pulling guard. I quit the team saying to myself, "I hate this stupid sport and all the bruises and pain that goes with it. I'm for sure not going to labor anonymously in the line blocking for someone else."

In the section on meditation in Chapter Six, the RAIN (recognize, accept, investigate, nurture) technique will be explored. It is a technique I use often. My most anxious time of day comes in the morning usually after during that last hour of sleep, when my eyes are still closed, but the monkey has started his chatter about whatever one or more things may be causes of worry at the time. The more difficult ones are those when the monkey starts his work at 3 a.m. after a bathroom visit and we're having to listen to him for the rest of the night.

Our first reaction is usually to push it back or resist. One of life's most important lessons is to learn that what we resist persists. The resistance magnifies it and creates another layer of stress.

The first step in taming anxiety that holds you back is to recognize when you're feeling overly anxious and try to dial it down. The first sign that it is becoming an issue to be managed will be a body sensation -- a knot in the stomach, shoulder tightness, etc.

Our success in life, whatever our goals and aspirations are highly dependent on managing our self-talk. My own anxiety, a thorn throughout my life, yet has helped me immeasurably anticipate obstacles, remain cautious where appropriate and stay organized.

Fear and stress properly managed are assets, as they furnish the fuel and energy to our dreams, aspirations and goals in life. When chronic and acute, they become debilitating and increasingly fatal. This book is meant to provide tools and methods to properly manage that part of our lives and provide real-life inspiring examples of people just like each of us that have struggled yet used these tools to turn what was debilitating into a positive driver in their lives.

THE MONKEY MIND AND THE ZOO

CHAPTER ONE

*Pink Floyd, "there's someone in
my head and it's not me"*

The Monkey Mind

We're all given these two gifts at birth and managing the monkey becomes our life's greatest challenge. It chatters incessantly with a lot of self-limiting stuff. Peace of mind and emotional balance is found in "being here now"—living in the present moment. The monkey and all the incessant mind chatter is always in the past and the future—regrets about the past or things that would have been done differently with the benefit of hindsight, and anxiety about imagined future events.

> *I spent most of my life worrying about things, most of which never happened.*
>
> **—Old man on death bed**

Monkeys are cute, unless we're talking about the one in our heads that talk and chatter incessantly, become lethal to our ability to achieve our dreams and ambitions, and get joy from our lives. Managing our monkey and the racing mind is our single biggest life challenge and the single greatest determinant in how far we go in life and, more importantly, how much joy and life satisfaction we achieve.

I Worried
Mary Oliver

I worried a lot. Will the garden grow, will the rivers
flow in the right direction, will the earth turn
as it was taught, and if not how shall
I correct it?

Was I right, was I wrong, will I be forgiven,
can I do better?

Will I ever be able to sing, even the sparrows
can do it and I am, well,
hopeless.

Is my eyesight fading or am I just imagining it,
am I going to get rheumatism,
lockjaw, dementia?

Finally I saw that worrying had come to nothing.
And gave it up. And took my old body
and went out into the morning,
and sang.

. . . .

It is the ultimate self-help topic. There are estimates that the average person has approximately 60,000 random thoughts per day, many fleeting and disconnected from any coherent theme. The pace of life in the digital age and the addiction that many of us have to our digital devices and multitasking exacerbate the problem.

In fact, the addictions run well beyond the digital one and include substances that are killing us in record numbers. In excess of 220,000 are dying annually in the U.S. from alcohol, opioid, eating disorder and suicide. This is the equivalent of 16 Boeing 737 crashes per week in America. There will be profiles in each chapter of "lives changed, and lives saved" by the adaption of the regimen outlined in Chapter Six.

The Zoo and Our Biggest Life Bully

In the Wizard of Oz, the Good Witch Glenda cautions Dorothy about the need to stay on the Yellow Brick Road on the way to the Emerald City and the Wizard. She mentions wild animals and wicked witches who live there in the shadows and prey on those like she and Toto. The human mind is similar in that the voices are often dark and foreboding. Our "biggest bully", the one thing that can handicap us for life—our self-limiting beliefs--those voices in our mind that are constantly sabotaging our dreams and hopes for a better life. These often come from events in life when someone expressed a very negative opinion about us or said something really demeaning that we have internalized and has become part of our accepted life narrative.

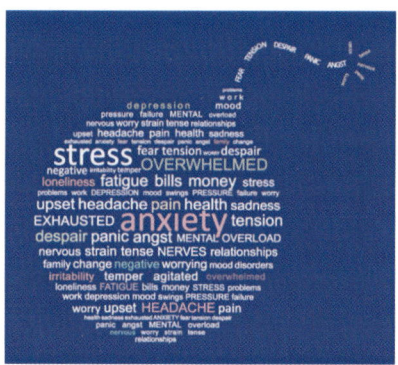

Self-gaslighting is a form of imposter syndrome. Self-rejection with thoughts of wanting things that you feel you're unworthy of, such as a new relationship or a job that your inner voice keeps saying things like, "I don't have the experience, the education or the social skills for that." Some sexual assault victims have talked years later about, thinking that maybe they brought it on themselves. Most of us are familiar with the concept of gaslighting, made famous by the movie of the same name, but have never considered that we might be doing it to ourselves with our self-talk.

Briana Bragg and Self-Gaslighting

"What you say to yourself in the mirror matters.

We talk to ourselves more than anyone else. By the time we are 40 we have 60,000 thoughts or more that run through our mind daily.

That's 60,000 internal conversations we have daily.

Most of them we aren't even aware of.

I used to have body image issues. 😟😫

When I would look at myself in the mirror, I would say things like:
"if you lost 10 pounds you would look great in this outfit"
And
"Damn, those are some serious dark circles under your eyes, did you get any sleep?!"

I uncovered through deep healing work this went back to my teenage years when I was bullied by my peers for my voluptuous curves.

I also used to be pretty mean to myself with the dialogue I had throughout the day.

When I would make a mistake, I would call myself an idiot or refer to myself as ditzy. (While I do have ditzy moments, I'm far from those connotations).

Do you ever catch yourself saying mean things to you?

Through practicing #awareness of myself and #selfmastery I learned about my inner critic.

I began discovering ways to shift the conversation I have with myself. Because I no longer wanted to live in the prison I had built in my mind.

How did I evolve these conversations?

- ✦ I use affirmations daily.
- ✦ I sing to myself in the morning "Good Morning Beautiful"
- ✦ I learned to laugh at myself... when I have a "ditzy" moment I laugh -- sometimes really hard, at what I do. I genuinely find myself funny.
- ✦ I empower myself during challenging tasks using phrases like "come on Bri you've got this"
- ✦ I tell myself that I'm beautiful inside and out and believe it.
- ✦ I surround myself with people who love me for who I am, not people who are trying to change me.
- ✦ I breathe deeply, and release fully when emotions of unworthiness come up.
- ✦ I talk about my insecurities rather than avoid them.
- ✦ I learned to quiet my mind with #meditation and being comfortable with stillness.
- ✦ I express how I feel authentically with honest integrity.

Did it happen overnight?
   No.

Was it easy?
   Hell No!

Is it freeing?
   YES! 🦋

I let go of the mind body connection that kept me judging myself against my past and against others.
♡ ✦ 🦋 & you can too! ♡ ✦ 🦋

I no longer ask: Are they going to like me?
I instead ask: Do I like me?
                Do I love me?

#valentinesday2022 is Monday... rather than seeking external validation for who you are this year, choose you.

Make the decision to like and love you.
All parts of you. 💝
Even the shadow side of you is part of you and it's ok. Be you. Love you.

When you do you find personal freedom from the cage of stories we tell ourselves, we become happy within our inner being. No one and nothing can take this away! 🦋♡✦ "

The most important step to take in identifying and coming to terms with the thoughts that are creating the emotional reactions is to recognize, accept, investigate and nurture the thought. This is a technique known by the acronym of RAIN. It is explained further in a later chapter. It rests upon the premise that what we resist will persist. Instead of judging yourself and feeling guilty for having the thought, identify it, call it out by name, and allow it to be present while you investigate it and determine its validity. I use this anytime I notice a knot in my stomach, or some other body sensation brought on by thoughts of some future event -- events that are almost always magnified beyond any real threat they pose to my actual well-being.

These toxic beliefs, which afflict us all, telling us we're not worthy, we're not enough, and how our dreams are all way too grandiose for someone of our limited skill and ability. These crippling beliefs affect both men and women but seem to be particularly acute among women.

Jacqueline Hayes[*]**,** Three-time author, motivational speaker and empowerment consultant

"Many women waste their time defining themselves through the eyes of others. They are looking for answers to questions that must come from within. They are seeking acceptance

---

[*] Jacqueline Hayes is an author of *"Unfolding: A Woman's Journey," "You Are Enough: A Guide to Love, Joy, Peace, Freedom, and Acceptance," "Blossom: Discover the Beautiful Flower Within,"* and *"Inspired Living: Beautiful Inspirational Quotes for the Journey."* **Website:** https://bit.ly/3aKlbis **LinkedIn:** https://www.linkedin.com/in/jhayeschangeagent

and approval from individuals who do not have the power or insight to give them such information." *You Are Enough, A Guide to Joy, Love and Peace by Jacqueline Hayes*

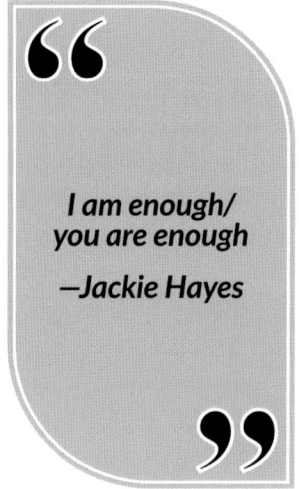

I am enough/ you are enough

—Jackie Hayes

Like so many who have discovered their life-calling, the source can be found in their life story. There is an adage, "to understand the woman, learn about the little girl." Jacqueline was a daddy's girl, and heartbroken at the age of seven when he passed away. "Who's going to tell me I'm beautiful, that I matter, that I'm worthy?" All these questions came and endured for a long time.

"My mother, heartbroken like me, now a widow and without skills for the outside world, grieving, depressed and staying in bed all day." PTSD was an undiagnosed condition then, but that's what it was for her. Jacqueline, was ambitious and driven to be something special and to matter, yet, when alone, and without a male authority figure in her life, "my thoughts were about my goals, but something kept holding me back. Was I enough? Did I have what it takes?"

"After college, driven by my ambition to make something of myself, I got a big corporate job that required client entertainment, with all the wine and bad eating habits that went it. Diet Dr. Pepper and Cheetos became my go-to when in a rush, which was most of the time. My body started rebelling. My stomach was constantly churning. Doctors couldn't find what was wrong, so they just prescribed medication. I had an advanced case of burnout and knew I had to make a change."

"The medication had failed, and I discovered on my own that a change to a plant-based diet with a more regular sleep regimen were good first steps. I added a regular practice of yoga, and meditation. This made the difference I was looking for. I decided to make the leap from my job to my calling, and I have never looked back." She wrote her first book, *Unfoldings: A Woman's Journey by Jacqueline Hayes*, and has written three more and become a full-time speaker and empowerment consultant. She recognizes that her challenges are those faced by all of us and has dedicated her life to helping guide others to a more fulfilling life of balance and equilibrium.

Women and Their Particular Challenges

Donna Ashworth: Author of *Ladies Pass It On* and three books. Poet and author from Scotland

Men don't age better than women,
men age without fear,
without worry,
without judgement.
Men age secure in the knowledge that it's as it should be,
and the fight is not theirs to take on.
Men age without prying eyes looking for lines,
looking for grey hairs or spare fat.
Men just age.
Freedom looks good on them, doesn't it?

Women age with the eyes of the world upon them,
lest they be considered to have let themselves go,
or lost a battle in the war.

Women age with the rules and restrictions,
of dressing correctly for 'their age',
employing new make-up techniques to hide drooping eyelids,
and steer attention away from the wrinkles.

Women age with the burden of beauty and the expectations of society,
wearing them down and creating even more pressure than before.
Making it harder to look 'well'.

Men don't age better than women,
they age without guilt.
It's worth a million new lotions, potions or pills,
promising youth.

Let's try it and see,
if freedom looks good on us all.

"I'm less than, I'm not enough, I'm too old, too fat, too thin, not smart enough, unlovable", and the list goes on. The monkey works 24/7, never takes a vacation, a day off and never takes a nap. These self-limiting beliefs that get hard-wired into our minds and become the never-ending voice of the monkey rob us of life satisfaction and in far too many cases lead to the perceived need to self-medicate with pills, alcohol, binge-eating and other health destroying substances. In cases like these, when traumas have created PTSD and other crippling mental conditions, the mind can become a complete zoo with lions, tigers and other man-eating animals.

Teen Stress and Anxiety at all-time high

The teen years have been difficult for all of us. The social media age has added a new layer, an often-overwhelming layer to the challenges young people of this generation face. The statistics on mental health among young people are truly alarming.

An alarming number of them are suffering from depression and dying by suicide. In fact, suicide is now the second leading cause of death among young people, surpassed only by accidents.

After declining for nearly two decades, the suicide rate among Americans ages 10 to 24 jumped 56 percent between 2007 and 2017, according to data from the Centers for Disease Control and Prevention. And for the first time the gender gap in suicide has narrowed: Though the numbers of suicides are greater in males, the rates of suicide for female youths increased by 12.7 percent each year, compared with 7.1 percent for male youths.

There is a serious mental health crisis for the youth of America, according to Dr. Vivek Murthy, surgeon general of the United States. There is a mountain of evidence supporting this.

These children and adolescents are bombarded with a toxic mix of vicious social media and harmful violent video games, television shows and films. In addition, this is the only advanced nation in the world where going to school has turned into a form of Russian roulette.

The discordant state of politics guarantees that nothing will change for these unfortunate youth. Our culture, which emphasizes winning at sports, egotism and accumulation of wealth, creates a weakened society unable to comprehend and deal with its most serious problems. The Covid pandemic is exhibit A.

Sonia Dhingra, Freshman at Williams College and Former Summer Intern at the Brain Performance Institute, University of Texas at Dallas

As a high school graduate and rising college student, I know that keeping my mental health in check is a necessity as I juggle the pressures of grades and social life. My question is: how? Even though I am fortunate enough to have attended schools that puts an emphasis on ending the stigma around mental health, I notice that my friends, classmates and I are constantly struggling to find ways to cope with stress and lead healthy lifestyles.

Teen girls struggle with complex social and academic pressures, and often times, schools and families are inconsistent in the ways they provide guidance, if they provide any at all. Oftentimes, adults underestimate the amount of pressure we are under, saying things like, "wait until you are an adult." Actually, a survey from August 2013 shows that many teens also reported feeling overwhelmed (31%) and depressed or sad (30%) as a result of stress.

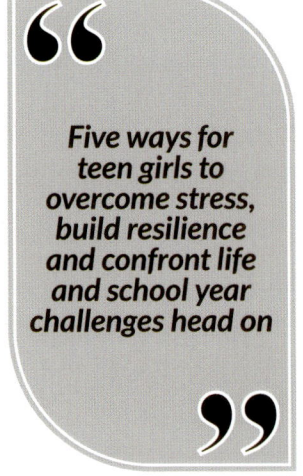

Five ways for teen girls to overcome stress, build resilience and confront life and school year challenges head on

More than one-third of teens reported feeling tired (36%) and nearly one-quarter of teens (23%) reported skipping a meal due to stress, according to the American Psychological Association. This makes sense due to the fact that most of the approximately 20 million teen girls in the US (not to mention those of us living across the globe) have to deal with social and family pressures, school, college applications and more. Yet, most of the mental health advice my friends and I encounter is perceived as preachy or irrelevant. Of course, it would be great to take days off and postpone assignments and spend my days doing what truly makes me happy. Nevertheless, this is inefficient in the long run. A lot of my friends have mentioned that chilling out too much in school ends up hurting students even more. They need tools that they can use in their everyday lives. Luckily for me, I've had the opportunity of interning at the Brain Performance Institute, part of the Center for BrainHealth at the University of Texas at Dallas, for two summers. The work my team (the Stress Solutions team) did on creating life-enhancing programs is important to many groups of people – ranging from the Dallas Police Department to war veterans to corporate executives – and to teen girls.

I've learned that our brains are neuroplastic, meaning that depending on how we use our brains, we can increase our connectivity, reasoning ability and more. One way to strengthen your brain and cope with stress is to build resilience. Resilience is not bouncing back from an obstacle but rather adapting to and healing from a stressful situation. One tool we can use to build resilience and cope with stress is mindfulness. Mindfulness is a form of mental training in which individuals engage in exercises to cultivate an attentive, present-centered, non-reactive mental mode. During my time at my internship, I went from thinking about mindfulness as a "nice-to-know" to a "need-to-know" tool that is backed by hard science. Research has shown that mindfulness can enhance human performance in terms of cognitive performance, physical health, brain health, emotional well-being, quality of life and situational awareness and attention.

Whether you are just beginning to feel the stress of high school or have been struggling with it for a while, here are five tips on how to practice mindfulness. Each of the five practices listed below is grounded in scientific research with measurable outcomes:

1. **Be grateful** – Gratitude means focusing on what you have, instead of what you do not. Intentionally showing gratitude activates the areas of the brain that are associated with emotional processing, social judgment and decision-making. In addition to the benefits on the brain, practicing gratitude can bring greater balance to life by reducing symptoms of anxiety and depression and strengthening social and personal relationships. In a 2012 study, group of Chinese researchers looked at the combined effects of gratitude and sleep quality on symptoms of anxiety and depression. They found that higher levels of gratitude were associated with better sleep, and with lower anxiety and depression. Feelings of gratitude directly activate brain regions associated with the neurotransmitter dopamine, or the "reward" neurotransmitter. To practice gratitude, some suggestions are to keep a gratitude journal, reflect on what life would be without certain blessings, savor the happy surprises in life, write an email to someone who has had a positive impact on you and visit someone you appreciate.

2. **Practice meditation** – At the Max Planck Institute in Germany, brain imaging demonstrated that brain structure actually changed as a result of different forms of mindful practice, including different types of meditation. Meditations can be guided or unguided. There are many different types of meditation, including breath awareness meditations, sound meditations and body scanning. When practicing meditation, your mind will wander. The practice of noticing the mind wandering and bringing your attention back to the breath takes practice. To practice meditation, find an app that works for you and remember that consistency is key.

3. **Practice mindfulness formally** – Think of practicing mindfulness formally as a gym for your brain. Not only does it help change your physiological response to stressors, but it also helps reduce mind wandering, which in turn makes you a happier individual. In fact, research at Harvard Medical School proved that mindfulness changed the brains of depressed patients. Practicing does not have to take very long. Some examples of formal practice are mindful movement and deep

breathing exercises. A tip for practicing mindfulness is to find something that works for you.

4. **Use Heart Rate Variability** – By using your smartphone or a heart rate tracker, you can measure your physiological response to stressors. If you can learn to control your heart rate variability, you will be a better decision maker, be more socially aware, have a better reaction time, as well as be more physically healthy. It is exciting to think that even though our emotions such as anger, anxiety, and more often get the better of us, there are specific strategies that we can all learn which will help us become calmer in the face of stress by bringing our heart rate back down.

5. **Practice mindfulness informally** – Informal practices can take place during those moments where you are truly present. This could be when you are working out, playing an instrument, observing nature, being present in a conversation, washing dishes and more. Informal mindfulness practices reinforce the formal practice and allow us to find meaningful ways to integrate awareness and richness into the rhythms of our lives.

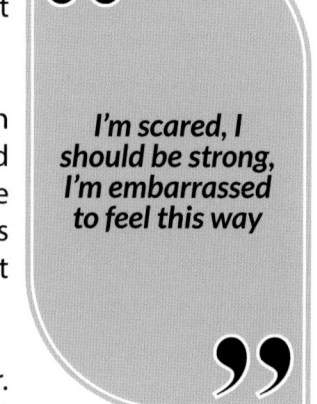

As teen girls around the world can achieve their full creative potential in both their social and academic lives. Here's to being our most positive selves."

The monkey can be especially brutal when we face situations that make us fearful and anxious. We often feel that this shows that are weak and cowardly. We convince ourselves that we are alone in feeling this way, and that we just need to "suck it up."

I'm scared, I should be strong, I'm embarrassed to feel this way

Fear is a natural, healthy response to danger. The amygdala in the brain is triggered and can be lifesaving during extreme circumstances. Carl Jung, the Swiss psychologist said, "What we resist, not only persists, but it also grows in size." Trying to push it away and being in denial about being scared only creates more anxiety and self-doubt. Being scared to death and saddling up anyway is courage, according to the famous movie cowboy, John Wayne. Managing our fear starts with recognizing it for what it is and acknowledging to ourselves that we are afraid. Managing fear successfully requires the willingness to accept and understand that courage begins with accepting it an facing it for what it is. There is a technique outlined later in Chapter Six in the section on meditation called RAIN (recognize, acknowledge, investigate and nurture) which can be very effective in converting scary situations into manageable ones.

It means we have the capacity to see clearly and sedate the monkey while we deal with the situation at hand. It means we have enough balance and equilibrium to not panic when things go off the rails.

It takes courage to be with things as they are. And that is what meditation teaches.

"Courage is being scared to death, but saddling up anyway."

- John Wayne

RAIN and other meditation techniques teaches us how to "saddle up anyway" and be with both the fear and pain. When there's pain, hardship or discomfort our hard-wired tendencies are to resist: to fight it, to look for someone to blame, to turn and run the other way, or to just shut off altogether and avoid it.

Stress, properly managed is good and is essential for success in life. Setting goals and feeling the pressure to do the things necessary and on schedule to achieve them is what gets us out of bed in the morning and on our way. It becomes debilitating when it is more than we can process and manage. It can be managed, and this book will show you how to achieve physical, mental, and spiritual well-being and balance. Happiness, or mental balance and equilibrium are available only through a regimen of mind fitness.

CHAPTER TWO

THE MONKEY AND OUR THREE AGES

"Stress is gasoline on the fire of aging."
Dr. Kara Alexander

"For lack of a nail, the shoe was lost
For lack of a shoe the leg was lost
For lack of leg the horse was lost
For lack of the horse the general was lost
For lack of a general the war was lost"
Euripides

O ur everyday choices about sleep, food, exercise, meditation time, social interactions and nature bathing are the biggest influences on our physical health and our biological age

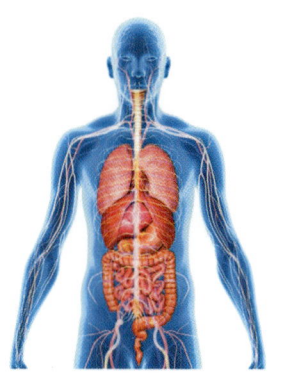

Mind/Body Connection

Undigested Stress: Sickness and Aging

This chapter is devoted mostly to the groundbreaking and not well-understood impact of chronic stress and anxiety on how we age. More understood is the impact on our physical health, so just a short few paragraphs on that as a refresher.

In his book, *The Unseen Body*, Dr. Jonathon Reisman refers to the "ecology of the body." He steps back from the individual parts to show the interconnectedness of the whole, and how the process of *homeostasis* is designed to keep it all in balance. The complexity of maintaining homeostasis becomes orders of magnitude more difficult as we age. The human body, he says, requires good plumbing to keep the flow moving through all the proper pipes to the right body organs. "Without good plumbing mental health deteriorates."

The body has been referred to as one big "chemical stew." There are 109 separate body chemicals in this stew and 22,000 genes that make up our genetic code. The years go by, the pace of life increases; we eat more, exercise less, sit more at our desks, go home to sit and watch television and self-medicate with alcohol. Sitting is considered by many in the medical field to be the new cigarette and tobacco-like habit.

This is a toxic combination. The effect on our organs and overall physical health has been long understood and written about. The effect on aging is more recent and the science behind it is Our digestive system processes and passes through the food and drink we ingest—not so for our emotions.

There is a direct link between our thoughts, emotions, feelings, and the physical impact on our physical body and organs? If your heart, lungs, liver, and other vital organs are getting a constant transmission from your brain of stress, anxiety, and depression, the physical toll over time can be enormous and lead to premature aging and early death. This can be the difference between vibrant health and so much of what ails all of us, both physically and mentally. Suffice to say, it can become a matter of life and death, and it is, in fact, becoming a matter of "death" for many.

Heart disease is still the leading cause of death in the United States with one person dying every 36 seconds from heart failure. A recent study, titled *Interheart,* tracked 24,767 patients from 52 countries. It found that patients who experienced a high level of psychological stress during the year before they entered the study were more than twice as likely to suffer a heart attack during an average follow-up of five years, even when traditional risk factors were taken into account. Its overall conclusion was that psychological stress is an independent risk factor for heart attacks, similar in heart-damaging effects to the more commonly measured cardiovascular risks.

It all starts in the brain's fear center, the amygdala, which reacts to stress by activating the so-called fight-or-flight response, triggering the release of hormones that over time can increase levels of body fat, blood pressure and insulin resistance. Furthermore, as the team explained, the cascade of reactions to stress causes inflammation in the arteries, fosters blood clotting and impairs the function of blood vessels, all of which promote atherosclerosis, the arterial disease that underlies most heart attacks and strokes.

> "
> *Aging is a disease— the most common disease—one that not only can but should be aggressively treated.*
>
> *David Sinclair, PhD (Lifespan, Why We Age and Why We Don't Have To)*
> "

Aging and My Story

"Age is just a number." This cliche, which I used to find amusing, is testimony to one of life's great adages that cliches become cliches because they are largely true. I read Deepak Chopra's book, *Ageless Body Timeless Mind*, soon after it came out 25 years ago. He said that we have three ages, not one, and that our chronological age, dating from our date of birth, is the least important of the three. Our DNA age being the most and followed by our attitude toward life.

He further cautioned against our self-talk with things like, "I can't do things that I used to be able to do, when I was younger, or my knees hurt too much, or I'm slowing down." He said this is an open invitation for the old man or woman to just move in and set up shop -- a self-fulling prophecy. That really resonated with me, and I have lived accordingly ever since, including irritating some of my closest friends with frequent reminders that such comments are "old man or old woman" talk. The book by Dr. Chopra was one of the great Eureka moments in my life. We all read and absorb some of what we read, incorporate some into our lives, but, as the years go by, much is lost or forgotten. Then there are those books or experiences that are among the great eye-openers in our lives. That book was one of those.

There are several more recent books and studies that have put forth the science, *epigenetics* behind the DNA age concept. Without a particular personal regimen, I have always exercised, slept well, eaten healthy (since college), and maintained a wide circle of friends (social networks). I hadn't heard of the Six Pillars for a large portion of my life, but intuitively understood a lot of what is now seen as this system.

My own struggle has been mostly with the food part. Regarding nutrition, I grew up in a blue-collar family with a dining regimen that was heavy on southern comfort food, with all the carbohydrates and unhealthy fats that go with that. I later learned that too much of even healthy food can really add the pounds.

My nickname in college was Goat and for good reason. A young local entrepreneur in Waco, Texas where I was a student at Baylor University, made the fatal mistake of opening a pizza parlor directly across the street from the freshman dorm. As an enticement, he offered two large pizzas free, if you could eat both at one sitting. I dined there 3-4 times a week. He finally closed, and I never knew if I was the sole reason, but my friends all blamed me. Until my metabolism went into permanent exile at about age 45, I could always exercise off the excess pounds. My Body Mass Index (BMI) remains above the norm for my height.

Twelve years ago, I added yoga and meditation to my regimen. I was so excited a few months ago to see an ad where you could order a DNA age kit, fill out a questionnaire and send three blood samples, and get back your actual DNA age. I couldn't wait to get back the results. Since reading the Chopra book, 25 years ago, I had believed, although without validating evidence, that one's age had more to do with factors other than your actual birthday. About 6 weeks later, I got the results back, and it showed that my DNA age was actually 68, a full 12 years younger than my chronological age. This made me younger than 99% of those my same chronological age, according to the report I received. As an aside, my wife, whose birthday is 18 months younger than mine has always joked that she was married to an older man. Needless to say, I took great joy in reporting this finding to her and, may I add, she has gone strangely silent on this topic since.

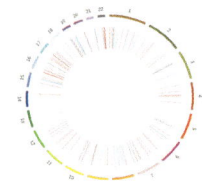

my DNAge

What is the DNAge® Test?

The DNAge® robustly detects epigenetic changes to determine biological age based on the aging clock built by UCLA professor Dr. Steve Horvath. Epigenetics is gene regulatory information layered on top of DNA. The reversible and dynamic nature of epigenetic marks makes DNAge® an ideal test to monitor lifestyle interventions.

Understand your DNAge®:

What is Epigenetics?

Your DNA isn't your destination. The reversible, dynamic nature of DNA methylation modifications (in contrast to genetic changes) make the DNAge® clock an ideal test to directly monitor lifestyle interventions.

"Why Your DNA Isn't Your Destiny" Time, Wednesday, Jan. 06, 2010.

Do you know that your diet and lifestyle will affect your DNAge®?

A joint study of 11 universities shows that a high plant diet with lean meats, moderate alcohol consumption, physical activity, and education benefit your DNAge®.

Epigenetic clock analysis of diet, exercise, education, and lifestyle factors. Aging.2017;9:419–46.

Is it true that women live longer than men?

By analyzing more than thousands of samples, scientists show that men have higher epigenetic aging rates than women in blood, saliva, and brain tissue.

An epigenetic clock analysis of race/ethnicity, sex, and coronary heart disease. Genome Biol.17 (1): 171.

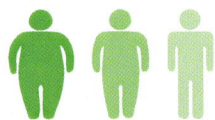

BMI: Not Only a Number

The fact that obesity accelerates epigenetic aging of human liver strongly suggests that BMI index and DNAge® may be significantly associated and become indicators of aging rate.

Obesity accelerates epigenetic aging of human liver. Proc Natl AcadSciU S A.111: 15538–43.

Learn more about the epigenetic clock and understand your DNAge® today at
www.mydnage.com/learn

Epimorphy, LLC

 **myDNAge**

Name: **Alan Steelman**
Sample ID: **UR910864**
Sample Collection Date: **Mar 7, 2022**

Sample Type: **Urine**
Report Date: **Apr 18, 2022**

1. Current Test Results

Based on the methylation value of your sample, your DNAge® is **68**.

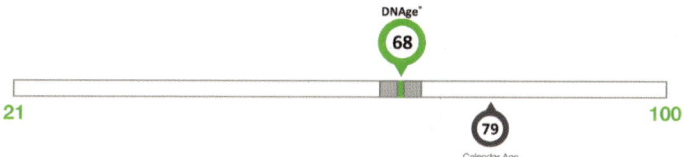

*Gray bars indicate the median of 2 standard deviations of replicated tests, showing the reproducibility of test.

2. DNAge® Index

Your DNAge® index* shows you are at 99th percentile of your age.
It means you are younger than 99% of people at your age.

*DNAge® index is calculated based on the current available database. It is subject to change with increased population.

3. Your DNAge® Compared to General Population

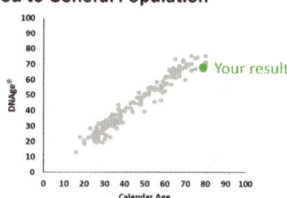

4. DNAge® Monitor

This is your first DNAge® test. To monitor your DNAge® changes, our scientific advisors recommend retesting 6-12 months after your original test.

Epimorphy, LLC

V 1.2

You Can Get Younger!!
Dr. Kara Fitzgerald: Younger You

Kara Fitzgerald, ND, IFMCP, is the first-ever recipient of the Emerging Leadership Award from the Personalized Lifestyle Medicine Institute in recognition of her work on DNA methylation. As a leading voice in the intersection of nutrition, epigenetics, and aging, Dr. Fitzgerald's work has been featured in media outlets such as Prevention, Fast Company, MSN, Everyday Health, and many more. Receiving her doctorate from National University of Natural Medicine, she is on the faculty at the Institute for Functional Medicine

"You can be younger tomorrow than you are today" Dr. Kara Fitzgerald

I will summarize this recently released book by Dr. Kara Fitzgerald in order to give you a flavor of what I consider to be a landmark and by far, best work on this topic to date. More importantly, I highly recommend that you buy it. It's loaded with practical steps to not only abate biological aging, but to even reverse it by as much as three-and-one half years.

She backs it all with the research and scientific evidence necessary to make a compelling case for what she recommends. The science is necessary to demonstrate the proof-points of her claims, yet, it is, as she says, "A layperson's guide and tour of aging and the science of aging, Epigenetics." Her mission is to not only help us deal with many of the debilitating effects of aging, but to also have more years of high-function living -- a longer, healthier life.

- Aging is a complex process influenced by many factors. Two people can have the same chronological age, yet their life expectancy and living quality can be vastly different. That's because, in addition our chronological age, which can only move in one direction, we also have a *biological* age. This bio age can actually move in reverse.
- Your biological age is affected by damage and degradation from both internal and external sources. By assessing your biological age, it can be determined how old your tissues, systems and even genetic material is. Your chronological age could be 50, for example, and your bio-age could be ten years older or ten years younger.
- The regimen she provides doesn't require medication, only changes in diet and lifestyle. Food, sleep, exercise and relaxation. You don't have to be already in some stage of relatively good health or fitness. At her clinic, many of the patients have chronic conditions -- autoimmune diseases, chronic allergies, autism, diabetes, cardiovascular disease, Alzheimer's, Parkinson's, etc.
- More energy, better mood, less depression, fewer headaches, lost weight, improved digestion are all results from many of the subjects at her clinic and the control groups who have been tracked during their time on the eight-week program outlined in the book.
- The recent trend for life expectancy in the United States has declined for three consecutive years. It's not just a shorter time, it's that we're spending more of our lifespan dealing with serious disease. Our lifespan can be physically, emotionally and intellectually vigorous until shortly before its close.
- The *Younger You* program aims to postpone chronic illness and the associated prescription drugs, surgical procedures and poor quality of life.

In the book, you will get the practical step to take:

- List of nutrient-rich delicious foods
- Foods to avoid that negatively contribute to aging
- Recipes and meal plans
- Lifestyle practices, including sleep techniques, exercise and meditation
- How to minimize exposure to things that can profoundly damage the epigenome and hasten the aging process

As Dr. Fitzgerald says, "Stress is like gasoline on the fire of aging."

Better sleep, food choices, exercise, meditation, social networks, and nature therapy all contribute to emotional balance and equilibrium, and surprise! surprise! surprise! An actual reduction in your DNA age, the most important of your three ages: A Younger You.

Food and Aging:

Want to Live Longer? Stop Eating Like an American. This headline from an article in Daily Beast is brutal and direct, but, hard to argue with given that the United States is second only to Mexico in global obesity.

It turns out diet might play a more outsized role than we thought in our aging process. A new peer-reviewed study published in *PLOS Medicine* suggests that a young adult living in the U.S. could add more than 10 years to their expected lifespan simply by pivoting away from a typical Western diet and closer to a traditional Mediterranean diet. That means eating much less red and processed meat; and eating many more legumes, whole grains, and nuts.

"Food is fundamental for health, and global dietary risk factors are estimated to cause 11 million deaths and 255 million disability-adjusted life years annually," according to the study.

You could live more than a decade longer by eating more plant-based foods.

Their key findings:

- Eating more legumes, whole grains, and nuts, and eating less red meat and less processed meat, increases life expectancy.
- The greatest increase to lifespan was seen in the 20-something age group. Males saw an average increase of 13 years and females almost 11 years.
- People in their 60s saw an increase of an average of 8 additional years by making the switch from a modern Western diet to the more-plant based diet.

It has been long accepted that what we put into our bodies has a dramatic impact on our overall health, no matter our exercise and other habits. Even he of the Hippocratic oath (first, do no harm) Hippocrates noted, 'Let food be our medicine, let medicine be our food.

There are a number of recent studies and reports suggesting a high intake of whole grains, vegetables, fruits, nuts, and coffee and reducing the intake of red or processed meats.

On average, it's the last sixteen years of life that present the most challenging for seniors. Making a change even during the proverbial golden years can reverse much of the damage done. The eight-week regimen outlined in Dr. Kara Alexander's book, *Younger You* profiled in this chapter is worth reviewing for anyone wishing to make the change.

Young people, who have resilience to poor dietary habits, get the biggest boost to added longevity according to the Norway study, with an added eleven and one-half years.

Red flags

There are warning signs that diet is starting to take a toll: brain fog, difficulty concentrating, or an afternoon low that impacts your performance can signal that it's time for a change, a need for coffee, sugar, or energy drinks to become functional in the morning, by noon, or to continue through your afternoon.

It is never too early and never too late for anyone for anyone who is motivated to make simple nutritional changes that have powerful and often life-changing effects on both long- and short-term health

You will find more detailed guidance and suggestions in Chapter Six in the nutrition section of the Six Pillars. A succinct summary is to move away from animal proteins (meat) to protein provided by plants. For example, having a chickpea burger instead of a cheeseburger. Fish, such as salmon, along with a diet that's more focused on fruits, vegetables, legumes, nuts, and seeds.

Without knowing this or having any specific regimen I was following, in the ensuing years following my "goat" period, I moved more and more away from red meat to fish, vegetables, nuts, fruits and a lot of what is listed here in this study. This has undoubtedly contributed to my DNA age referenced above.

Aging and Exercise:

In a recent study done a group of British scientists, a group consisting of dozens of males and females between the ages of 55 and 79 were recruited. They had been cycling for decades, and still pedaled about 400 miles per month. None were competitive athletes.

An original 2014 study found them to have reflexes, memories, balance, and metabolic profiles that more closely resembled those of 30-year-olds than of a similar sedentary older group.

A newer study recently published in Aging Cell, they decided to look further into other factors including muscle and immune systems.

The two sets of scientists then dove into their data, and both concluded that older cyclists are not like most of the rest of us. They are healthier. They are, biologically, younger.

Their muscles generally retained their size, fiber composition and other markers of good health across the decades, with those riders who covered the most mileage each month displaying the healthiest muscles, whatever their age. The impacts on riders' immune system also were marked. In the older sedentary people, the output of new T cells from the thymus glands was low. The inactive older peoples' thymus glands also were atrophied, compared to those of the younger group.

The aging cyclists, on the other hand, had almost as many new T cells in their blood as did the young people. Those who exercised also showed high levels of other immune cells that help to prevent autoimmune reactions and of a hormone that protects the thymus against shrinkage.

More and more evidence that aging is both a disease and is both preventable and reversable.

SURFING THE STORMY SEAS/WHAT CONDITION OUR CONDITION IS IN

In 1978, the First Edition released "Just Dropped In" (to see what my condition is in). This was long before the internet, social media and many of the other things which contribute to today's crisis, and while it is likely that the lyrics are describing a hallucinogenic trip of some sort, they could as easily be describing a current life of despair, born of burnout, broken dreams, or one of the many other causes leading to this global epidemic of stress and anxiety.

The best of times and the worst of times

At the macro level times have never been better. In his recent book, *Enlightment Now*, Psychologist and Author, Steven Pinker provides ten reasons why things have never been better for mankind. Among these: the percentage of the world's population living in extreme poverty has plummeted since 1950, homicides and deaths from war have decreased significantly, life expectancy has been rising, more countries are adopting democratic forms of government, etc. In addition, the amount of information available with one simple click on a digital device has never been greater, the number of creature comfort options available online obviates the need for taking the time to spend hours at the shopping mall, and the list goes on.

The obvious problem is that none of us live at the macro level. Our lives and the conditions of our existence play out daily at a dizzying pace for most, where dreams and lives are being pursued and for many falling short and falling into lives of despair.

The mantra for life in America, for much of its history has been "bigger, better, faster, stronger." This has served us well at the national level as the country has succeeded on virtually all fronts: economic, culturally, militarily and standard of living for most. It has also provided an unprecedented platform of opportunity for advancement without the class barriers that exist, even in the first world countries of Western Europe, where accent, going to the right schools, etc. still govern so much of an individual's ability to advance. A disclaimer is in order regarding the United States, where race and gender discrimination still exist, but, relative to that of other countries are much less a factor.

"The American Psychiatric Association tracks mental health issues and reports periodically. The increase is staggering. Pre-Covid, reported anxiety among adults rose 38 percent in 2018. Nearly 20 million reported a major depressive disorder, including three million adolescents ages 12 to 17. Nearly 20 percent of the adult population, approximately 60 million report anxiety issues. The really sorrowful reports concern suicide.

Despair the American Dream and Burnout

"Only the strong survive" was recorded by Elvis Presley and others and the song is about a young man jilted by his sweetheart, and his mother is telling him to get off his knees and hold his head high and get on with his life.

This advice happens to be the personal mantra of many who consider themselves strong and competitive, and yet, reach a breaking point or a burnout point that indeed does bring them to their knees. In a "bigger, better, faster, stronger" rat-race competitive environment the race to reach the top too often becomes a fall to the bottom. Too often pride won't allow them to seek help and the consequences are becoming increasingly fatal. Suicides in America last year were 44,000.

A survey of 1,500 U.S. workers, done in 2021 showed more than half said they were feeling burned out as a result of their job demands. The "great resignation" as it has been termed refers to the aftermath of the Covid pandemic and the decision by many to either leave the workforce entirely or to take the time to find something that was less stressful and more in line with their interests and skill set.

Burnout as evidenced by the life stories in this chapter manifests both physically and mentally. Feelings of helplessness and cynicism often come to mind, along with physical symptoms of insomnia, loss of appetite or the reverse—a need to binge eat. Physical exhaustion, nausea, gas, indigestion, and headaches are all possible warning signs that should be flagged, and action taken to mitigate. The central message of this book is that chronic stress is a killer and burnout can often be a way-stop on the road to something far more serious.

Don Drake: PTSD/West Point/Banking: Burnout and Life Saved

There are many stories of PTSD in the lives of veterans returning from the combat zones in both Iraq and Afghanistan in the wake of the 9/11. Don Drake's case is military related, but not combat related. "I was traumatized growing up and well before getting to West Point. My brothers, my mom and I experienced quite a bit of trauma growing up, from my father who had a major problem with rage and stemming from that, a lot of verbal abuse, and physical abuse, very serious physical abuse." Thankfully, he and I have reconciled, and he has really changed his ways, but the years in between were nightmares for our family. I knew from as early as the second grade that I wanted to go to West Point. I honestly think part of what attracted me to the military was I thought perhaps there would be no emotion there."

"It would just be order, structure and the business of becoming a first-rate American warrior. and there'd be no room for emotional reactions to events. I was not disappointed. Though happy with my time there, I knew that this wasn't my life calling. Things from my childhood were still lingering. I had anger, depression, a lot of fear, an awful lot of fear. The panic attacks were particularly debilitating.

Out of the military, went to SMU, got my MBA and graduated there in 2001, and started my banking career with a focus on the oil and gas industry. My career really took off with four promotions in a year. I was doing big deals and my external world was functioning at a very high level. Joining a second and larger bank, I completed a $50 million deal, one of the biggest ever for this particular bank.

This should have been a time of really big elation, yet I was still struggling with that darkness inside. I was medicating with alcohol. I had been a top 10% performer in everything I did including and my business career, and yet, no satisfaction, no lasting satisfaction in the end.

To make matters worse, I was treating my body as a machine to be driven, rather than as the sacred container for Spirit that it is, meant to be nourished and cherished. I was working very long hours, seven days a week often, smoking, consuming large amounts of stimulants and energy drinks as a replacement for sleep, eating junk food as another form of self-medication, and feeling restless if I was not working.

The stress-related deaths from alcohol, drugs and suicide in 2018 alone exceeded 200,000, and is equivalent to 22 Boeing 737 crashes per week. As horrific as the school shootings, hurricanes, tornadoes and fires are, the deaths from all these events pale in comparison to the stress-related death rate

As a result, I broke my body twice -- once by driving it to go into atrial fibrillation requiring several days' hospitalization, and once by knowingly (and foolishly) placing it repeatedly into a dangerous situation resulting in hydrogen sulfide poisoning, a terrifying feeling of suffocation and vertigo, and a brush with death resulting in another hospital stay in a small west Texas oilfield town.

Interestingly that second body-breaking brought me face to face with my mortality and I made some serious changes in my life -- I began eating a healthy diet, which for me was lower-carb, primal style diet, beginning a deep and devoted practice of meditating and energy healing, which involved lots of time in nature and with nature -- and brought me into several sanghas, or communities, of like-minded spiritual seekers. I lost some 55 lbs., and as I felt better, I began to work out routinely and now believe I am in better shape than I was in my 20's at West Point!

On that journey back to health, I found my life calling, which is "leading people to the truth of who we are so that we can be free." I now regularly conduct energy healing sessions and teach meditation to individuals and groups of young men who are seeking a deeper meaning in life, am building community, and have had many mystical experiences in nature which prompt me to go deeper and explore further

The pursuit of the dream, and the "bigger, better, faster, stronger" mantra that American's have grown up with for past generations, provided a level of job satisfaction and economic reward that met the expectations of most and a life that certainly had its rocky parts, but didn't create the despair that seems to be the most prominent feature for too many today.

The Misery of Success and the Misery of Failure

The burnout from an unrelenting pursuit of the "dream" can be just as debilitating as the despair of failing, it seems. America's mental health crisis is most pronounced among both many of the most successful and those who feel they've failed and have given up.

It should also be noted that the "burnout" phenomenon is not exclusively an American one. The only other country that equals if not exceeds the drive to succeed in America is Japan. There is even a word for it, *Karoshi,* which literally translated means "overwork death." If the drive in America springs from the promise of the American Dream, the drive in Japan is largely attributable to the nightmare of its humiliating defeat in WWII. The "loss of face", which is a central feature of Japanese life, the rubble left from the bombing of Hiroshima and Nagasaki, and the crippling financial reparations it was forced to pay all taken together create an unrelenting drive to overcome all this that endures to this day.

Karoshi hotlines are in place throughout Japan to help people cope with this condition. Interestingly, many of the calls to the hotline come from the wives and family members of workers suffering from what might be called secondary *Karoshi*. In 2018, an Expedia survey found almost 60 percent of Japanese respondents felt guilty for taking a vacation, and a sense of guilt about leaving the office even after long overtime hours.

Super Moms, Doctors, lawyers, Wall Street: In her new book, *Mommy Burnout,* psychologist, Sheryl Ziegler says too many mothers are running themselves into the ground trying to be super moms. Most of the attention and commentary on the helicopter or bulldozer parent is on the stress they are causing their children, yet the stress created on themselves is equally palpable.

Dr. Beth Funk: Wonder Woman Burnout

As with most who grew up in an Army family, Beth Funk attended 10 different schools from Kindergarten through 12th grade and graduated from Marymount International High School in Rome, Italy. She is a graduate of the University of Texas at Austin with a degree in Elementary and Special Education, she also holds a master's degree in educational administration and a doctorate in educational leadership. Beth worked in public education for many years, and also spent several years teaching psychology and professional development at Blair

Junior College in Colorado Springs, CO, and as an adjunct professor in the College of Education Graduate School at Kansas State University

For those of us who think we're pretty special, but not quite super-hero status, Beth Funk's story will give reassurance that even Wonder Woman can take on too much and crash and burn. She has been an advocate for holistic living, another way to describe the Six Pillars, for as long as she can remember. She discovered that her regimen was missing one important dimension, which turned out to be truly life changing.

As one would expect for someone like her, the "crash and burn" didn't result in any addictive behaviors, but was more than a two-year painful, challenging recovery period.

A dedicated and competitive triathlete, three teen-agers at home, her husband, General Paul Funk deployed to Iraq, casualties occurring in units under his command, pursuing her EdD studies, and employed in an administration position in the public school system. She had been a practitioner of most of the Six Pillars her whole life. "I just kept plugging forward, she says, and thinking that I was dealing with it pretty well."

The crash came in the form of and intensely painful debilitating back injury. "I had always been active in sports, stayed active, ate properly, and followed a regimen that I thought would always ensure top performance in all of my pursuits."

This dedication to excellence is not surprising, given the discipline that has been a part of her life since birth. She grew up in an army family. Her father, the late Lieutenant General John Yeosock was in charge of all ground forces during Desert Storm. She has been an army wife and professional educator for 35 years. Her husband, Four Star General Paul Funk was base commander at Fort Hood, the world's most populous military base, until his promotion to Commanding General of TRADOC, the Army Training and Doctrine Command at Ft Eustis, VA.

The debilitating back injury and its aftermath changed her life dramatically. "I couldn't think of anything I had done to cause the type of damage that I was experiencing." I spent two full years pursuing the cause and a cure through the more traditional mainstream paths of medical doctors, chiropractors, spinal injections, etc. Layered on top of the physical pain, was the anxiety, constant worry and inability to sleep, I was even having to stand to eat my meals, the pain of sitting was so intense. None of these brought relief.

Through the influence of my daughter, I decided to try yoga. I had no idea that it was the accumulated stress that had caused the injury. The stress management benefits of yoga, when all else had failed, brought the "Eureka" and she has never looked back.

She is on the frontline in a number of ways in helping American military service members and their families cope with life marked with stress, anxiety, and uncertainty. "As human beings", she says, "we crave stability." In the military, there's little stability, given the re-postings taking place all the time, the overseas deployments and the anxiety faced by the family concerning the safety of their deployed loved one.

Coming out of her life-changing experience with yoga, she founded the Life Moves Yoga Studio at Ft Hood in Killeen, Texas. It has been enormously successful, necessitating a move to a larger facility in Harker Heights. The demand has created a need for more certified instructors. She and her daughter, Amanda created a Yoga Teacher Training Academy. Given the diverse population at Ft Hood, the offering ranges across all ages, including seniors, doing chair yoga. PTSD is a big issue in the military and there are special sessions to aid in post-trauma growth. Free classes are offered through a non-profit, they organized for active-duty military, first responders, and schoolteachers.

Like so many, who have experienced a life-changing experience through yoga, she has become an evangelist, converting not only others, but, her own family members, who experienced first-hand her transformation. Her husband, General Funk is a practitioner and a strong supporter of her efforts. Her 82-year-old father-in-law and mother-in-law have become disciplined practitioners in their own right. Her son, Nate, a recent university graduate, decided his passion was the same as his mother and his older sister, and is a certified personal trainer, yoga instructor, nutrition coach and weight-loss coach. Amanda, the original influence on her mother's life changing experience continues to instruct and co-manages the studio. This is a family truly serving their country and others in a life-changing transformative way.

Addressing Burnout In Your Own Life

Ignoring the symptoms especially in our culture, is the path taken by too many. Better self-care and management of stress and anxiety is without question the best preventive measure. Consulting a healthcare professional is the best first step when the warning signs of burnout are all flashing red. Given that up to 95% of cancers and other potentially fatal diseases and conditions are the result of chronic stress, these conditions can sometimes have advanced to the point of requiring medical treatment.

Dorsey Standish

An ennobling life purpose discovered amidst a traumatic episode, and a purpose devoted to the biggest life challenge we all face. Equipped with a hard driving type-A personality and an engineering degree from an Ivy League university, she was on a fast track to a very successful and financially rewarding career at Texas Instruments, a Fortune 500 semiconductor and integrated circuits company. She describes her career plan as well-mapped: get into a large corporation, climb the ladder, take on as much as she could as fast as she could and reap all the benefits of a fast rise to the top.

Her drive and talent didn't go unnoticed. She was promoted to program manager very quickly requiring a lot of international travel. She spent her 25th birthday in Taiwan, a global center for semiconductor design and production. "I remember feeling on top of the world and really thought that I was doing everything in my power to be happy and successful."

Then came the "crash and burn" that same month right after her 25th birthday with a full-blown case of stress-induced burnout. This required a two-month medical leave in order to recover both her mental and physical health. Taking a hard-look at her priorities gave birth to a new life's calling and what she considers to be her true purpose.

Managing stress and anxiety is a lifelong challenge for everyone. In the aftermath of the pandemic, stress levels are at an all time high. A recent survey by Feelmore Labs found that 63% of respondents said their stress and anxiety levels were worse than ever before. Poor sleep, loneliness, and physical exhaustion were mentioned by many as being hallmarks in their current lives.

Dorsey's career remains focused on "circuit boards"—just different ones—the ones in the brain and using mindfulness and emotional intelligence training to help with equipping her clients with the coping skills to better navigate their lives and careers.

She is the Chief Executive Officer at Mastermind, where she draws on her experience as a Neuroscientist and a Corporate Wellness Expert. Mastermind is a Dallas-based mental wellness firm founded in 2016 to bring science-based brain training techniques to organizations nationwide, including brands like Toyota, Staples, and American Airlines. It is a 100% woman-owned business whose purpose is to grow a happier, healthier, more compassionate world by equipping every person with an inner toolkit for mental wellness.

A speaker once challenged an audience of hard-driving, Type A business executives with a question that brought a quiet ambience to the room: "With your present workstyle, will you live to enjoy all the fruits of your labors?"

Dorsey says that she faced this same existential crisis in her own life. She and the Mastermind faculty see among many of their corporate clients, those who may not have heard this particular challenge, phrased exactly this way, but, intuitively see that they need to make a change in their work-life balance in order to avoid much bigger mental and physical health issues later.

The company's website offers a good summary of both the challenge we all face and the adjustment that is available to meet the challenge with more resilience, balance and equilibrium. "Change your thoughts, and change your world" is their call to action.

Dorsey says, "Our community and our world needs mindfulness and mental resiliency now more than ever. In a world of uncertainty, what is certain is each moment, each breath, and the ability for each person to find their own inner peace. We believe that in today's challenging, everchanging environment – made even more uncertain by COVID – Mastermind can help people manage uncertainty, connect with their own inner strength, and ultimately thrive in their personal and professional lives."

Her personal transformation and passion for brain health has even converted some of her once-skeptical family members. "My dad is a very successful lawyer who runs the insurance practice at a major Washington, D.C. law firm. Work causes him a lot of stress. He checks his email first thing in the morning and last thing at night, priding himself on his responsiveness to clients, but I've seen over the years many times that he gets hijacked by this stress and anxiety. When I first got into yoga and meditation, my parents didn't really get it. My dad would put his clasp his hands at his heart and say, "Namaste" with some silly chanting when I brought up the practices I loved so much. Over the years, I've seen a shift in their hearts and minds. Both my parents have both seen what a big impact mindfulness practices have had on me, and they have become more open about trying meditation. My mom now uses the Calm app regularly, and my dad took weekly mindfulness classes with me and the Mastermind team during the pandemic. He often quotes my teachings back to me, with "Change the Channel" being his favorite tool for switching from negative thoughts to a more neutral topic (just like you would hit a button a TV remote to change what you are experiencing).

This family transformation parallels her current mission at Mastermind: to share science and experience with Type-A skeptics to turn them into believers and practitioners of mental wellness on a regular basis. One mind, one heart, and one inner toolkit at a time, the Mastermind team works towards a happier, healthier more compassionate world.

Chronic stress can have a variety of causes — financial problems, relationship woes, and caregiving burdens, among other things. The burnout among mothers during the home-schooling period during the pandemic, among schoolteachers, nurses, doctors, and other caregivers was an epidemic unto itself.

For those who haven't reached the point of needing medical care for their condition, the regimen outlined in Chapter Six which explains the Six Pillars of Well-Being is the best and most effective antidote for reaching a point where medical attention is necessary.

THE MONKEY GETS VERY LOUD/STRESS-RELATED PERFORMANCE SUCCESS AND FAILURE

M anaging the game both inside and outside the lines is a daunting challenge for all of us. We all have three lives: public lives, private lives and secret lives. We perform at work to the best of our ability, put our best face of confidence and self-assurance on and go about our work. Our private lives at home and our secret lives are for many where the self-destructive habits of self-medication take place with both food and other substances are used to cope with our feelings of stress and inadequacy.

Both the amateur and professional athlete have to have a skill set that allows them to perform on the field and successfully compete on the day of the game. This has always been the case. What is new is the time off the playing field or outside the lines, where they are for the first time in history having to deal with cable news networks and social media criticism of their performance.

Many of us live our lives vicariously through the exploits of our heroes. The stories that have started to emerge recently about the stress, anxiety, and pressure of the lives they actually lead, have shown that they may be endowed with exceptional physical gifts and skill, but struggle with all the same mental challenges that the rest of us do.

Goose Gossage: Baseball Hall Of Fame and Fear on the Mound

The great Yankee pitcher, Goose Gossage, on a panel of former major league baseball stars said recently that he was "scared to death" every time he took the mound. He was one of the pioneers in what today is called the "closer." The pitcher who comes in during the late innings to "save" the game, often with runners already on base, and a stadium full of screaming fans depending on you to send them home with a win to celebrate. This is particularly a challenge in certain cities like New York and Philadelphia where the hometown fans are especially unforgiving of failure.

There were a large number of young high school and college players in the audience and Goose singled them out with a lot of his commentary. One particular comment which really struck home with them was him saying that most who reach the major leagues are not very far apart in physical skill and ability. Those who succeed are those who can manage the game between "their two ears" where all the performance-failure demons dwell. The three other panelists, Andre (the Hawk) Dawson, Jim Edmonds and the Mad Hungarian, Al Hrabosky all echoed the same message, and shared stories of their own struggles.

The monkey plays no favorites and in fact is often more punishing to those whose physical gifts allow them to rise to great heights in their chosen field.

Little foam rubber toilets: flush it!

A method for major league baseball teams developed by Brain Cain widely regarded as the foremost authority on mental performance mastery is the little foam rubber toilets to flush bad at bats and little foam bricks to toss away when the mental load of a performance failure becomes a load too heavy. Baseball at the major league level with its daily games may be an easier task to off-load than the other major sports where there is a several-day lapse between games and the burden of the "choke" or mental lapse has to be carried for a longer period of time.

In most cases these athletes are still very young and not very developed in the social and emotional learning skills necessary to manage that side of their lives. This adds an order of magnitude new level of stress to their lives. Equally, those who have jobs and careers have a game inside the lines and outside the lines to manage.

There's no media criticism to deal with, but still the stress and anxiety of relationships with colleagues and a difficult boss and a toxic work environment can create a perceived need to self-medicate with alcohol, pills, or food and in many cases cause one to verbally abuse loved ones out of sheer anger and frustration that was brought back home from the office. Managing the stress to perform at a high level, whether at the office or on the athletic field, can be equal to, if not greater than mastering the particular skill set to perform.

For the athletes and teams that we cheer for, we are entertained and live vicariously through their performance on the playing field. Their successes and failures are there for all to see. Less visible and understood are the factors that matter the most in achieving the competitive edge.

Top Performers and the Competitive Edge:
The monkey gets very loud

**Flavio Ungaro, Chief Executive,
Mentally Fit Institute, Latin America**

Flavio Ungaro was born and grew up in Italy, played professional basketball for 9 years then coached for another 4 years. Drawing on lessons learned from both his successes and failures on and off the field as a professional athlete, he is now a businessman and applying these lessons to a different playing field, but one equally competitive. He holds a Masters in Mental Preparation for Top Performers and is now CEO of the Mentally Fit Institute for Latin America. This is a global company, headquartered in Brussels, and applying lessons learned from sports and how top performers in business and the professions can achieve the competitive edge.

He says, "I Have lost, I have been benched, I have choked multiple times during my career. The monkey gets very loud in stressful game situations. Fortunately, a fisherman, a soldier and a basketball player taught me the secret of success: the greatest of all capacities is to learn from what happens to you so you can make it happen the way you want."

The learnings about human performance failures have many parallels and lessons that are applicable to the hyper-competitive playing field of business today. The example of the athlete is easy to grasp, not as much for the business or professional person—the client base for the Mentally Fit Institute. The playing field for the businessperson is more competitive than ever. The playing field or competitive landscape is global for most companies now. The competitor, their product offering, their pricing etc. are often halfway around the world with competitive advantages that require more agility than when competitors were more local and easier to analyze. "It is ever-changing, complex and very ambiguous for most", he says.

Because of the pace, complexity and ambiguity, the competitive edge is more in the mind, the mental agility and the choices made than ever before. Mind fitness is key. The technology that we have now enables less dependence on manpower, yet requires better leadership, and more informed decision making. Many companies who thought technology was the answer to productivity lags and invested many millions in ERP systems have found themselves doing the wrong things faster.

Creative Destruction, the process of old business models and products being made obsolete at a faster and faster pace is a threat to the very survival for those companies that are slow to adapt. The playing field has dramatically changed and the importance of being able to remain calm and think rationally in the face of the speed of change today is certainly an important key competitive edge.

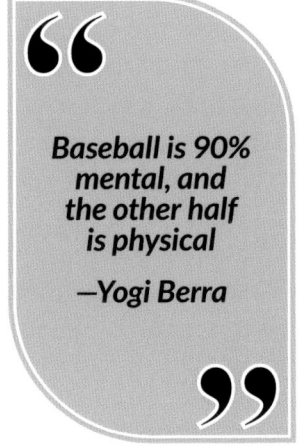

Baseball is 90% mental, and the other half is physical

—Yogi Berra

The key to mind fitness is a regimen of self-care. This is the key to maintaining the balance and equilibrium necessary for rational decision making and keeping pace with rapidly evolving marketplace changes.

The Mentally Fit Institute addresses the issue at three different levels within the client organization: individual, team and corporation: Fit to Play for individual (physical, mental, emotional fitness) Fit to Lead for managers Fit to Grow for the company or organization (purpose, pride in the mission and a team focus on achieving the mission).

For several decades, the focus on career advancement at the personal level, for many has been largely on getting the treasured MBA degree. This does enhance the skill set in many ways, yet, just as on the playing field of the elite athlete, the skill set gets you on the playing field, the ability to manage the stress and pressure of the game between the lines most often determines the outcome.

Mental Skills Coaches for the Mind
26 of the 30 major league baseball teams employ sports psychologists like Brian Cain (profiled above).

Bigger, better, faster, stronger

We all experience some level of stress and anxiety leading into some high stakes' events in our lives, athletes, business executives, public speakers, high profile TV, news anchors on all of us in America, that "bigger, better, faster, stronger" is the true path to success. This mantra has served us well as a country, as it has led to dominance in many areas and a level of prosperity not enjoyed in most other parts of the world. It has also, been the mantra of the U.S. Military. The dark side of this for the country, our civilian population and our fighting men and women is that it has led to an unprecedented level of mental and emotional damage. It may come as a surprise to many of our listeners that the U.S. Military, the world's finest fighting force, including our elite Special Operations Forces have discovered that "bigger, better, faster, stronger" isn't enough in today's environment and that yoga and meditation has been added to the training regimen, and is being used widely to better equip our commanders and our soldiers with the mental and emotional skills to deal with the rigors of battle and life afterward.

Jamie Alden: Green Berets, The Fog of War and Yoga

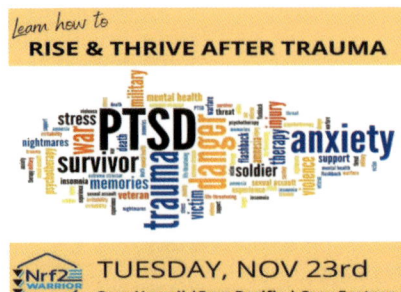

The stress and anxiety of those in the military, especially those in the elite special forces deployed to combat zones is palpable. The Fog of War has been used to describe the chaos after the first shots are fired and the noise, smoke and blood engulf those on those both sides. A commanding general once said that no battle plan lasts beyond the first shots being fired. "Keep moving, shooting and adapting until the smoke clears", he said. Managing a racing, anxious mind in the midst of an engagement that could take your life is a challenge unlike most any of us will experience.

Retired Special Forces Lieutenant Colonel, Jamie Alden, a West Point graduate, served 4 combat tours over a ten-year period in Afghanistan, and experienced these conditions first-hand. He is the quintessential American warrior in the finest sense of that term

During his four different deployments, he learned an important lesson after being upbraided by one of his subordinates in the aftermath of an engagement with the Taliban. The Staff Sergeant, a sniper under his command, screamed at him for his lack of patience and leading the small group too quickly into the engagement.

"After the mission was complete and we were loading our vehicles to go back to our base camp, he gave me a piece of his mind. He was furious and frustrated. Questioned my judgement, leadership skills and understanding of our mission."

He was correct. If it wasn't for the personal practice that I had developed and continue to develop to this day, I would have been unwilling and unable to reflect on my actions. I knew I needed to redeem myself and through the use of meditation and other mindfulness tools I had learned much earlier, I was presented the opportunity to respond, rather than react. And, a few days later, we were able to capture several of the enemy fighters without a shot being fired."

Jamie and his wife, Susan are both graduates of West Point, and he credits her with introducing him to yoga and meditation as 2nd Lieutenants during Officer Basic Course. Being a woman at the U.S. Military Academy in the earlier days following women being allowed to attend was an undertaking full of challenges in itself. She was sexually assaulted by a fellow cadet and in a separate incident, by a non-commissioned officer who was serving as a cadet mentor. She also had her shoes spat on by an alum as she stood in front of her company, preparing to march them onto the football field for pre-game festivities. The alum screamed at her and said, "You don't belong here. I was at West Point when the Corps was a real Corps... no women!"

In their post-military career, they live in Hawaii and have dedicated themselves to helping those crippled and traumatized by their military experience, their families and first responders. They founded and currently lead *Mind Body Aloha,* a wellness company that provides veterans, first responders, and people of all ages with the tools and resources to take control of their health. In addition to teaching yoga and meditation, they share unique offerings including revolutionary cellular activation products, nutrition guidance, workshops on Ho'oponopono and the Medicine Wheel, and transformative retreats for mind, body and spirit.

Mindset, says Jamie, is the single greatest challenge we all face in living a life of balance and equilibrium. To put another way, the *Monkey,* bombards us with distractions that are a constant impediment to our discipline and staying on the right path. Managing the mind to stay "here and now" is the simple, yet most difficult challenge we all face. They have both been to the foothills of the Himalayas on separate occasions to learn ancient wisdom for themselves and others. Jamie practices and shares Himalayan Kriya Yoga, in which he utilizes ancient breathing techniques within the Pranayama, Kundalini and Tantric traditions, which involve techniques such as "bellows breath", that will be understood by all those who practice med

The Other Playing Field: Top Business and Work Performance

The pace of life in general due to all the factors of life in the digital age is at an all-time fast pace. In the business and professional world, the days of the three-martini lunch are long past. There aren't enough hours in the day, given the pace, to allow for it, and the health robbing effects on the physical and mental health for those involved, like that for athlete, has finally been recognized.

There's no shortage of high-powered individuals with, what most of us would consider, high-stress jobs. A trend, started among Silicon Valley tech tycoons and entrepreneurial leaders is one of drinking green-infused smoothies, organizing office-wide yoga and meditation sessions and prioritizing balanced lives over ones spent living behind a desk. Their measure of financial success begins with the balance sheet. Many of them now have physical and mental wellness balance sheets. This just might be the modern-day secret to success.

Twitter founder and CEO Jack Dorsey's self-care routine is one of the most noteworthy, including intermittent fasting, ice baths and a daily five-mile walk to his office. He reportedly aims for at least two hours of meditation a day. And he's not alone.

Several of these leaders are embracing the practice of mindfulness through meditation. In addition to reducing stress, the practice has been proven to provide a sense of purpose, discussed at greater length in Chapter Six, decrease feelings of isolation and alienation... [and] symptoms of illness as diverse as headaches, chest pain, congestion and weakness.

Meditation is being introduced into a number of Fortune 500 companies. Harvard Business School Professor, and former CEO of Medtronic, Bill George, has said that "meditation gives me an opportunity to get deep rest and refocus before my board meeting." Billionaire tech mogul Marc Benioff of Salesforce has said that meditation influences how his leadership style. "Having a beginner's mind is critical today business. The beginner's mind allows me to step back so that I can create a new future, not what was.

And that's just one of the health-driven practices more and more movers and shakers have been adopting—not just for themselves, but for their companies as a whole.

At Salesforce, yoga classes are provided for employees twice a week. The CEO of GreatCall, takes his team surfing and organizes weekly yoga sessions. Mark Bertolini, the former CEO of Aetna introduced yoga to the 13,000 employees of the insurance giant. He has said that it not only increased communication and collaboration but also shed some light on the struggles his employees were facing, causing him to raise the minimum wage and improve their benefits.

When it comes to dollars and cents, the most important financial metric, physical health is the most measurable significant pay-off. Employee stress costs American businesses up to $300 billion a year, according to the World Health Organization, while 75 percent of all healthcare spending is on chronic illnesses that could be prevented. That's not to mention the hidden costs of sick days and lower productivity. At the end of the day, a business is only as healthy as the people running it, a fact that industry leaders are finally taking seriously.

THE MIND AND OUR BRAINS: THE SCIENCE

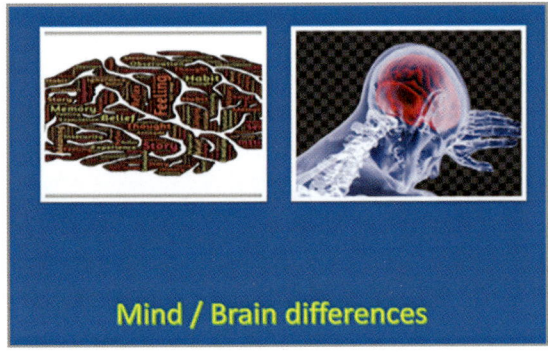

CHAPTER FIVE

Mind / Brain differences

The mind and our brains brain aren't the same. Brains. Plural you might ask. The brain behind our forehead is the one we traditionally refer to. Yet, the other two, our gut and our heart are often of equal importance, and both contain neurons, the key ingredient of a thinking organism. When weighing a potential romantic partner, they might get checkmarks on all your desired qualities, yet there is a nagging area of doubt that you keep feeling and you might say to a friend, "I really like him, but there's just something that doesn't seem right." There's the head voice and the gut voice. In romantic situations, there's also the heart voice: "I'm going to marry that person", so now two out of three are saying go ahead, and yet, the nagging doubt remains and grows. Then you hear the old adage, "Love is a fever cured quickly by marriage", and you finally decide to forego this one.

At the Wisdom of the Body Summit, Deborah Rozman, CEO of HeartMath, a scientifically validated system said, "People talk about listening to your heart, following your heart, go deep into your heart for the answer. And those metaphors can be found in every culture, almost every major religion. And those same cultures talk about qualities of the heart as love, care, kindness, compassion, forgiveness, respect, and more. And what we found through research—and our own experience, of course, but that science is now saying these aren't just churchy or sweet or religious qualities. These are emotions that actually activate the higher perceptual centers of the brain, and they lead to intuitive insight and more fulfillment."

In the 1990s, a discovery was made that spawned a whole new field called Neurocardiology. The finding was that the heart has a very complex nervous system that can sense, feel, learn, and remember. This little brain in the heart is actually independent of the brain in the head. "Cardiologists have been taught the brain controls the heart— the heartbeat, the heart rhythm, the blood pump.

"It's not true", says Rozman. "It's a two-way communication. And the heart is actually, through the vagal nerve, sending more signals to the brain telling the brain how the body feels and what to do, more instruction to the brain, than the other way around. In fact, 90% of the neural traffic between heart and brain is afferent, meaning the heart telling the brain what to do. And this validates what Aristotle and ancient Chinese said: that the seat of intelligence is in the heart."

Abraham Lincoln is his first inaugural address spoke of the "higher angels of our nature" as the voices that should guide us in healing the divided nation during the Civil War period. All the emotions that lead to acts of violence: anger, envy, lust, greed, etc. are products of agitated mind. Achieving emotional balance and equilibrium, the purpose of this book, can only be attained by reaching a state where all three of the brains are heard and given their proper weight, depending on the circumstances.

The other partner in this brain triad is the gut brain. "A primal connection exists between our brain and our gut. We often talk about a "gut feeling" when we meet someone for the first time. We're told to "trust our gut instinct" when making a difficult decision or that it's "gut check time" when faced with a situation that tests our nerve and determination. This mind-gut connection is not just metaphorical. Our brain and gut are connected by an extensive network of neurons and a highway of chemicals and hormones that constantly provide feedback about how hungry we are, whether or not we're experiencing stress, or if we've ingested a disease-causing microbe. This information superhighway is called the brain-gut axis and it provides constant updates on the state of affairs at your two ends. That sinking feeling in the pit of your stomach after looking at your post holiday credit card bill is a vivid example of the brain-gut connection at work. You're stressed and your gut knows it—immediately.

The enteric nervous system is often referred to as our body's second brain. There are hundreds of millions of neurons connecting the brain to the enteric nervous system, the part of the nervous system that is tasked with controlling the gastrointestinal system. This vast web of connections monitors the entire digestive tract from the esophagus to the anus. The enteric nervous system is so extensive that it can operate as an independent entity without input from our central nervous system, although they are in regular communication. While our "second" brain cannot compose a symphony or paint a masterpiece the way the brain in our skull can, it does perform an important role in managing the workings of our inner tube. The network of neurons in the gut is as plentiful and complex as the network of neurons in our spinal cord, which may seem overly complex just to keep track of digestion. Why is our gut the only organ in our body that needs its own "brain"? Is it just to manage the process of digestion? Or could it be that one job of our second brain is to listen in on the trillions of microbes residing in the gut?" *From* The Good Gut: Taking Control of Your Weight, Your Mood and Your Long-Term Health, *by Justin Sonnenburg and Erica Sonnenburg, PhDs.*

The brain is a biological organ that provides the computing power to process the all the sensory experiences. It has size, dimension, color and pictures and diagrams illustrate its constituent parts.

The monkey and all the drama that comes with him or her dwells in the mind—that mysterious hyperactive dimension of our lives that has no physical properties. Quieting the mind chatter and giving our three brains their proper weighting is the most important part of determining the direction, emotional balance and equilibrium, success or failure in our lives.

In a previous chapter, you read about top performing athletes and how the game is "played between the two ears", meaning one's physical skills gets you to the professional leagues, but your success once you arrive is governed mostly by how you experience and process the stress, anxiety, pressure and praise and criticism of fans, the press, and social media.

Briana Bragg:
Vacation of the Mind and a life saved

Nothing is more empowering to others than someone who is willing to lead by putting themselves and their life struggles "out there." Sexual bullying as a child by both girls and boys, heartbreak due to a failed relationship, and burn-out at age 27 are all hallmarks of her life.

In her own words, "I have overcome suicidal depression, chronic pain, chronic fatigue, financial hardship, a failed partnership, heartache, lost friends, yet have found that healing from all of this was available to me through my own inner healing process." As difficult as it is and has been to share these experiences publicly, she has come to recognize the value to herself and others by doing so.

No stranger to the power of change, she boldly and decisively stepped away from decades-old inner turmoil, limiting beliefs and subconscious patterns, along with self-doubt toward a personal awakening grounded in peace and light. Today, she likens her metamorphosis to that of a caterpillar in a chrysalis turned effortlessly into an agile butterfly.

Briana fully recognizes and appreciates the vivacious strength that awaits us all on the other side of personal struggle should we choose to capitalize on our challenges for transformation and growth.

Like the way a caterpillar breaks down in its cocoon so that a beautiful butterfly can emerge, she empowers women around the globe to transform their own lives and free themselves from their limiting patterns and obstacles.

The elevated consciousness she possesses is the direct result of intentionally aligning her present moment awareness of her inner thoughts with the ever-present, healing rhythms of the natural world around us.

As a young girl, Briana sought solace outdoors and embraced the synchronicity and flow of nature. From gardening with her much-loved Grandfather to observing the wonder of carefully collected and released caterpillars to butterflies, the beauty, simplicity, and wonder of nature were ever-present and healing during the tumultuous times in her early years.

As with all mesmerizing transformations in nature, Briana's freedom from what kept her grounded and small was not easily won or realized overnight. The balance and flow of nature cannot be harnessed or ushered into our spirits on demand. Instead, the dramatic and beautiful change occurs once we are open to growth and the desire for a synchronistic life.

She understands on a personal level how deep-seated feelings of fear, shame, and guilt drive people to recoil and withdraw from happiness and personal freedom.

From a childhood burdened with conflict at home and bullying at school leading to a fear of confrontation and struggle with setting boundaries in relationships both personal and professional, the inability to recognize her self-worth and value led to many challenges as she struggled to find her footing and purpose as an adult.

As a high achieving A-type personality, Briana had built a successful business in her early 20's through relentless drive, ambition, and perseverance. As with so many, nothing, including her own self-care was going to get in the way of her achieving her goals. This single-mindedness led to burn-out at age 27, and a total body breakdown leaving her bedridden for three months. She knew a change in her self-care rituals, limiting beliefs and mindset needed to happen, so she chartered a course for shifting patterns in her life that kept her unhealthy and stuck.

This evolution led her into her second business venture, Vacation of the Mind™, a company specializing in nature centered guided meditations with a certification for the process for those who want to teach the integrative methodology to align the potential of the mind with nature's abundant healing properties.

At the launch of her certification program and new company, Briana experienced a significant, traumatic life event that spiraled her into a two-year plight of chronic pain and a derailing experience with depression which temporarily sidelined her vision for a newly launched company and goals for the future. This depression led to a heart-breaking split with her partner of 4 years, which happened in the middle of the pandemic.

Although, taking her own life was considered on numerous occasions, thankfully she never followed through, and her story of recovery is an inspiring one. In addition, she emerged with a new mission in life -- lead and guide others who are struggling to find triumph through their challenges. She provides a safe cocoon where her clients can go through the breakdown to get to the breakthrough, much like a caterpillar turns to mush inside the cocoon before re-emerging as a butterfly.

After overcoming a two-year battle journey riddled with depression, she fearlessly and unapologetically redirected the course of her life's journey. Just as the butterfly emerges from a cocoon of destabilizing entrapment, Briana also metamorphosed into a spirit that values contentment, joy, and freedom.

She has moved her life from Chicago to, an idlyllic haven in Costa Rica ideal for health re-sets and rejuvenation. This international move by herself to an area filled with an abundance of nature's balm gave her space to not only to learn how to become fully self-reliant in a foreign place, but also to come to a full understanding of what she'd unconsciously sought after her whole life.

One exciting new venture underway is her is her Women's Initiative, focused on high-achieving business and professional women like herself. The objective is to equip them with the tools and techniques to achieve the proper balance between the overwhelm of their careers with the appropriate amount of self-care needed to thrive at life.

She manages her own monkey and self-limiting beliefs through a dedicated regimen of the Six Pillars and then some. 8 hours of sleep, a mostly plant-based diet, hiking, rollerblading and weight training for strength. Yoga and meditation are daily practices. The mind and body are inextricably linked, and yoga and meditation are key to centering the mind and maintaining calm. A network of friends and clients keeps her social network healthy and vibrant. A true believer in the benefits of nature therapy, she not only spends time in the forest, hiking and meditating, but is a believer in the benefits of hugging trees, often. She recognizes that some consider "tree hugging" to be a little weird, but also recognizes that "the path less traveled" is the path that makes all the difference in her life and that of others.

Her Vacation of the Mind concept is centered around being able to visualize a tranquil retreat to some distant and calm oasis where the mind can be centered and achieve balance through a consistent, dedicated meditation practice. Her business and movement are growing led and inspired by her own compelling life story and dedication to others.

Through the process she now teaches to others, Briana's past strife has transmuted into empathy, compassion, and self-respect effectively bringing her metamorphosis into fruition. By going within and embracing change, Briana learned to equalize, evolve, and become one with the universe's rhythm.

The message Briana wishes to share is a simple one -- as nature effortlessly navigates the ebbs and flows of time, so too can humanity.

As you confront the A.S.A.P.'s (anxiety, stress, addiction, pressure) in your life and find that coping is becoming more and more difficult, are you finding that you get relief, but only temporarily, from another pill, another shot of vodka, another cookie, or another session of retail therapy?

In the Wizard of Oz, as Dorothy started her trek along the Yellow Brick Road, she began to encounter others with a need to see the Wizard, whom they believed possessed the magical powers to grant their greatest wishes and make their dreams come true. First, there was the Scarecrow, who wanted a "brain" with which to think and make wise choices. Dorothy's entourage grew as they trekked along and encountered the Tin Man, who desired two things: A heart with which to love, and oil for his joints, which grew rusty each time it rained. Finally, as their destination grew closer, the group, full of hope, encountered what they thought was the most fearsome creature in the forest—a Lion, the King of the Jungle. When they recoiled in horror, he quickly said, "Don't be afraid. I know I'm supposed to be King of the Jungle, but I'm afraid, I'm a coward, and I need courage."

For you, a disciplined devotion to the Six Pillars in the real world will indeed provide oil for the joints (flexibility and strength), a calmer mind with which to make "wise choices, and "courage" by clearing your mind of the chatter and clutter, which hinders us from pursuing our dreams to "go for it."

Dr. Melanie Greenberg, Ph.D.

Fix your brain—fix your life!

The Stress-Proof Brain is more than a book that explains your brain and how it functions. It includes many practical tools to perform self-analysis and self-treatment. It can help you "rewire" your stress response to be more flexible, positive, and wise.

You should buy this book. Here are some highlights:

- "Many addictive behaviors such as drinking, smoking, taking drugs, overeating, and overindulging in shopping or sex are, at their root, attempts to avoid the uncomfortable emotions from stress."
- "Emotional eating is directly linked to cortisol levels and stress."
- "Studies show that persons under chronic stress can age prematurely, up to ten years sooner than peers."
- "Mindfulness has the potential to make not only individuals, but businesses, institutions and societies stress-proof."
- "Your breath is the most common anchor in learning and adopting mindfulness into your life."

- "Adult brains can be rewired through a process called neuroplasticity."
- "Mindfulness, practiced 30 minutes per day, can actually shrink your amygdala."
- "You can become the CEO of your own brain, keep your prefrontal cortex firmly in charge and make your brain less reactive to stress."
- "You can generate inner calm, build healthy lifestyle habits, and facilitate clear thinking."
- "A stress-resilient brain is the best thing you can have for staying focused, fit, connected, and on top of your game.

- Dr. Greenberg says, "If I had to choose one tool, it would be mindfulness."

You may see this as "going into the weeds" to start examining this connection and how all the body organs connect to and are impacted by us thoughts, beliefs, and emotions. To you and those earnestly searching for answers, such as:

- A mother or father of a son or daughter who overdosed, who are haunted by "where did we go wrong?"
- Someone, in a sober moment, asking, "How did my life go off the rails this way?"

Air-Traffic Control: The Prefrontal Cortex

To fully understand how and why "false wizards" become the default choice for many of us, it is necessary to understand something that most of us have never heard about or given any attention to. The prefrontal cortex, like air traffic control, is that part of the brain that lies just behind our forehead. As our eyes and ears take in the sights and sounds around us, we process with the prefrontal cortex what we see and hear, our thoughts about it, and weigh the consequences and make considered decisions on next steps. Have you wondered, "Why do I lose it sometimes for even the slightest provocation, or why did I react to that idiot on the expressway the other day, who cut in front of me? What if he had a gun?

The Hijacker: The Amygdala

The amygdala, located near the center of our brain, is part of our "threat system." Its job is to keep us safe by alerting us to danger. It is the brain's emotional" computer, unlike the prefrontal cortex, which is the logical computer. Unfortunately, it isn't very good at discriminating between real dangers "out there" and dangers we are just thinking about. It elicits the same response in both cases and can even be set off even by an unpleasant memory from the past, even though the danger has passed. If you are a trauma survivor, the "false trigger" is particularly problematic in extreme cases where trauma has occurred.

The prefrontal cortex, where calm, rational weighing of risk and reward takes place, can get "hijacked" and become flooded with cortisol. A recent case in point is that of Chris Kyle, a much-decorated U.S. Navy Seal from the war in Iraq. Kyle wanted to be of help to a fellow veteran and had taken him to a shooting range in Texas as an act of charity. However, he was killed by that fellow veteran, who was suffering from a severe case of PTSD. It was never determined what the trigger was in this case, and it is one of many recent cases where a returning veteran, traumatized by their service in one of our recent wars, has committed some inexplicable act of violence. The encouraging news is that the Six Pillars are proving to be very effective in helping trauma survivors, including more serious cases of PTSD.

Colonel June Copeland:
Wonder Women, West Point and a life-changer

L to R top row: 1st Lieutenant June Copeland, Colonel June Copeland, Bottom row: Cadet Jasmyn Copeland, Cadet Jeilyn Copeland

The life-changing "aha moment" that comes early for some and late for others -- the mind-body connection is credited by Colonel June Copeland, currently serving as Director of Business Systems Architecture, Department of Army, and a veteran of Operation Iraqi Freedom, and Operation Spartan Shield as, one that has finally equipped her to better navigate the stress and anxiety of her very successful, yet demanding military career. What an inspiring life story of a single mother and her three daughters, all West Pointers, and all aspiring toward very ambitious career goals of their own.

"I finally realize the necessity of both mind fitness and physical fitness and how they are inextricably linked. I've always maintained a disciplined physical fitness regimen. Walking, weightlifting, elliptical machine, etc. The endorphin high has always brought temporary, but fleeting relief." The military uses SOP (standard operating procedures) in everything they do. She says, "I finally have an SOP for managing my mind fitness."

After taking up yoga and meditation, she has finally discovered the magic in these two ancients, yet tailor-made practices for the most stressed period in our lifetime. She reflects on the physical ailments that plague some members of her own family and credits her physical fitness regimen with helping her avoid them. Yet, feels that in time, the undigested stress and anxiety of her life would take its toll on her, as well.

As a woman leader, commander and now executive, she faces all the challenges that women do, plus, additional layers. The military, a male-centric institution for all of human history, adds a layer, as does race. "I'm all about the mission and achieving the targeted objective", she says. There's a fine line to be walked between holding everyone accountable to their assigned duties and mission completion on time and having a style that doesn't come across as a "black woman with attitude."

She joined to do her job, she says, and when the lives of others depend on you, you must ensure that those who report to you are operating up to standard. Behavior for a male that would come across as standard military behavior can get a female of color marked as difficult. "I work hard to put on a face of empathetic understanding and not let my assertiveness to achieve the mission become a barrier to achievement.

I've had many wonderful experiences and comments on my leadership style. Unfortunately, the ones that linger with you are the others. After the feature cover article on me and my daughters appeared in the magazine, *Military families: West Point Legacy,* one comment was that this just proves that nepotism still lives and another one, that this now proves that racism doesn't exist any longer.

Growing up in Georgia, her family decided to stay on the same plantation where her ancestors had been held in slavery and where her grandmother was born. She was cajoled by her twin brother, at age 18 to enlist in the military. He served his enlistment time and returned to civilian life. She decided to make a career of it. Currently, she is at the Pentagon as Director of Business Systems Architecture. This follows deployments to Iraq, Kuwait and other missions in the Middle East and other parts of the world. She, like so many who are deployed to overseas assignments have to deal with the separation from children and other family members. The three girls lived with their grandparents during this time. Her daughters credit her, in spite of these periods of separation, to keeping them focused on the necessity of a good education, and for providing the example that they have all chosen to follow.

Colonel Copeland is grateful for having finally discovered the other pillars of well-being. She is concerned about her current state of sleep-deprivation, given the demands of her current assignment, but now that she has an SOP for the complete Pillars regimen knows that she will return to a full practice in time.

The "monkey"—and we all have one—resides in our prefrontal cortex most of the time and creates all the back-and-forth chatter as we go about our busy daily lives. While the chatter is distracting and robs our days of much of the joy and satisfaction we would otherwise enjoy, it doesn't become dangerous until the monkey gets scared by some event or trigger, and then jumps back to the amygdala and "starts screeching at the top of its voice." Even among otherwise emotionally healthy persons, incidents like road rage or a perceived insult in a social setting can set off a "hijacking" of the prefrontal cortex by the amygdala, meaning a flood of cortisol has occurred and the person will act in some rash way, possibly with tragic consequences.

The Six Pillars Magic!

Mentioned briefly in a preceding chapter, the *vagus* nerve is the most important nerve in your body! It is your body's interstate highway system or road network and is the key to understanding the magic of an integrated mind and body fitness regimen.

The feeling of calm, hydration, radiance, or even bliss that one experiences during and after a good night's sleep, a vigorous yoga session, for example or a vigorous walk in the woods. It is also the way to understand the toll that anxiety can take on the rest of our internal organs. It is among the many complexes, perplexing, and least understood features of the mysterious integrated human biological miracle: The human body.

This nerve branches out from the brain and connects to all the vital organs, wending its way throughout the maze of the body's organs and viscera all the way to the colon. Constant stress tips the balance toward a "hijacking" by the amygdala, thus promoting inflammation, hypertension, anxiety, insomnia, obesity, and accelerated aging.

Exercise, meditation, yoga, social networks, nature therapy, all stimulate the vagus nerve that carries information from the brain to all of the body's major organs. Most importantly, it also transmits those four naturals "feel good" chemicals you were given at birth (serotonin, dopamine, oxytocin, endorphins), which calm and slow everything down and allow self-regulation. News bulletin! Your happiness does depend on drugs. You've just been using the wrong ones! You have a pharmacy in your head! Use the ones given to you at birth. Okay, one final big word: Neuroplasticity! The stimulation of the vagus nerve makes rewiring of the brain, possible. If you are a PTSD survivor, or if you have a family member or neighbor who has suffered a trauma of any sort, this is good and encouraging news! This is particularly important to people with more advanced cases, such as trauma survivors. It is a process "that makes it possible to healthily increase the size, strength and density of our brains, just like physical exercise can make our muscles stronger and denser with more endurance" (Consciousness Research Institute).

THE BRICK HOUSE: THE SIX PILLARS AND SEDATING THE MONKEY

CHAPTER SIX

Matthew 7:24-27: *"Everyone then who hears these words of mine and does them will be like a wise man who built his house on the rock. 25 And the rain fell, and the floods came, and the winds blew and beat on that house, but it did not fall, because it had been founded on the rock. 26 And everyone who hears these words of mine and does not do them will be like a foolish man who built his house on the sand. 27 And the rain fell, and the floods came, and the winds blew and beat against that house, and it fell, and great was the fall of it."*

For those who employ the Six Pillars, awaiting them is a life of resilience and ability to adapt and even sometimes thrive in the midst of some of life's greatest challenges. The brick house and its ability to withstand the "rains, floods and winds" referenced in the book of Matthew is a good metaphor for the Pillars and what they provide us. Purpose is the roof and sleep is the foundation upon which the other pillars rest.

Purpose: The Roof

Your life purpose consists of the central motivating aims of your life -- the contribution you make to life. Purpose can be large, grand and noble like that which drove Mother Teresa, Desmond Tutu, Marin Luther King, Beethoven, Albert Einstein, or it can be less grandiose, but, unique and important to that individual and to society at large:

the family breadwinner, the parent and school teacher whose purpose is to prepare the next generation, the first responder, the doctors and nurses who persevered during the Covid pandemic, the senior, who in retirement years volunteers for a charity organization. The list is endless of the central motivating purpose that motivates us to arise each day and go about our lives with that stride in our step.

Purpose guides life decisions, influences behavior, shapes goals, offer a sense of direction, and create meaning. For some its meaningful, satisfying work. For others, their purpose lies in their responsibilities to their family or friends. Others seek meaning through spirituality or religious beliefs. Some people may find their purpose clearly expressed in all these aspects of life.

Purpose will be unique for everyone. what you identify as your path may be different from others. It often changes and evolves as we move life.

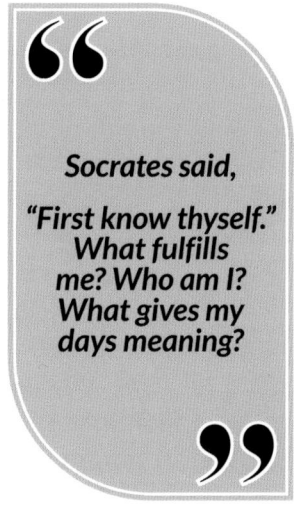

Socrates said,

"First know thyself."
What fulfills
me? Who am I?
What gives my
days meaning?

It may take the better part of a lifetime to discover our life's work, even though we may have been doing it our whole lives without necessarily realizing it. Our life's work is not always what we do to make money, although we often think it should be, and sometimes this way of thinking prevents us from seeing clearly what it is. It may be the work of having children, caring for them, and running a household. The way we know our life's work is by how we feel when we are doing it.

"When we are doing our life's work, we feel an uncanny sense of ease and alignment. This doesn't mean that the work is always easy, and it doesn't mean that it's the only work we have to do; it just means that there is a conviction deep inside us that tells us we are in tune with our innermost self. When we are engaged in our life's work, our bodies feel more alive, because our energy is devoted to a cause that, in turn, feeds us. We may be tired after engaging in our life's work, but we are almost never depleted. We feel grounded in the world, knowing that we belong here and have something important to offer." *Daily OM on Finding Our Life's Work*

When we are deeply unhappy, depressed, or subject to one illness after another, this may be due to a sense of disconnection from our life's work. At times like these, finding the work we are meant to do is an essential act of healing. Most of us remember a time when we felt fully engaged in some act of work, service or creativity, and it is here that we may rediscover the work we are meant to do now. On the other hand, it may be time to explore what inspires us through volunteering, taking a class, going back to school, or just doing whatever it is we long to try. We all have callings, and when we find them, we owe it to ourselves to nurture and protect them, because while they may or may not be our livelihood, they are the keys to our wellbeing.

Ways to Find Purpose:

What do you care about?
Purpose is all about applying your skills toward contributing to the greater good in a way that matters to you. So, identifying what you care about is an important first step. For younger persons, observing injustice and hardship by others can often be the source of finding their calling. For an older person, retired and feeling adrift, asking oneself questions like, what skills from my work life could be of value to a non-profit and what do I care about?

What matters the most to you
If your interests and experience cover a wide range of issues, writing them down and prioritizing them is a good first step. This should be followed by weighing your values regarding these issues and deciding which might require you to go beyond certain barriers that you consider important.

What are your strengths and talents?
We all have strengths and skills that we've developed over our lifetimes, Yet the monkey and the self-limiting belief chatter may make us unsure

of what we have to offer. What will I really enjoy? How can I leave my mark on the world?

Testing the waters by volunteering

Trying out new things and seeing if you really enjoy it and are my skills applicable to the needs of the organization and community. This has the added benefit of putting you in touch with others and getting the benefit of the social interaction. Some can work alone toward some larger cause, but most find a shared cause to be more energizing and inspiring.

Identifying role models and those we admire

Sometimes the people we admire most in life give us a clue to how we might want to contribute to a better world ourselves. As said before, your purpose doesn't have to be grand and large. Looking to your inner compass—and starting to take small steps in the direction is the best first act toward finding your true calling.

Sherri Doucette: Transforming Personal Pain into Medicine for Black men

"Baba's little roll of antacid tablets, seemingly harmless at the time, provided temporary relief to what, at age 44, unfortunately became stage 4 esophageal cancer."

The pain and grief, for Sherri Doucette, of losing her husband was almost unbearable, but gave birth to a cause she has devoted her life. Sherri recognized that his cancer was a symptom of a larger issue: the need for Black men to have access to resilience-building practices that have the potential to heal ongoing trauma and build sustainable resistance against oppressive systems and institutions.

The CDC says Black men ages 18-35 suffer worse health outcomes than any other group and have the lowest life expectancy due to structural inequities and racism that serve as greater health determinants than healthcare access.

"Death of a thousand cuts" (Chinese proverb): Navigating life as a person of color and the microaggressions that mark daily life take an enormous toll on mind, body and spirit. This is particularly acute among Black men. There are many examples among us all, of how chronic stress, derived from unending feelings of despair and hopelessness resulting from family dysfunction, traumatic life experiences, and other societal ills takes a toll on our physical bodies. The undigested stress illustrated in chapter 3, demonstrates that coronary vascular disease, obesity, diabetes and various autoimmune disorders are direct causal outcomes of the inability of many to process their stress.

Sherri understands the importance of a multipronged approach to wellness, therefore she incorporates all Six Pillars (sleep, nutrition, exercise, meditation, social networks, nature therapy) into her daily classes and wellness retreats. Yoga and Meditation classes are offered several days per week at different locations across the DFW metroplex.

Higher Ground is an annual retreat for Men of Color at a sprawling 80-acre ranch in east Texas where attendees are invited to explore restorative practices designed to raise consciousness and energy using nourishing whole foods, connection, breath, sweat, movement, meditation, and rest.

Wade in the Water is a half day experience, along Five Mile Creek in the southern Dallas area, developed following the murder of George Floyd. The title borrowed from the often sung Spiritual by enslaved persons planning for liberation. Its lyrics cautioning runaways to traverse riverbeds to elude slave patrols. In a much similar fashion, Black men were invited to the water for an emotional escape and an opportunity to release their collective despair, anger and frustration – together.

PREVENTITIVE HEALTH WORKSHOPS

Litehouse Wellness offers a variety of workshops to support health and wellness:

- Grocery Store Tours demystify healthy plant-based shopping.
- Shop Talk Men's Conference provides a safe space for conversations centering emotional, spiritual, physical and financial health
- Level-Up Your Legacy, a 3 part life planning series, offering legacy literacy and resources

THE PROOF

One of Sherri's yoga class regulars, a considerate and affable man in his mid 30s, called to check-in with her at the beginning of the pandemic quarrantine. He offered his appreciation for her teachings and shared just how impactful the practices had been for him. He admitted to Sherri that he had previously been abusive toward a romantic partner, but didn't recognize his behavior until a recent situation left him angry and seeking to lash out. It was in that moment, he said, that he recalled Sherri sharing about self-regulation - taking 90-seconds to connect with the senses before responding... It led to an awakening that for the first time left him contrite. He said he called the person that he harmed, apologized for past behavior and made a commitment to do and be better. He said that he was grateful for the increased self-awareness that developed since beginning his yoga practice with Sherri.

My Life and Times Adrift and At Sea

I have never lacked for knowing at various stages of my life what I felt my calling was at the time. Having said that, there are times in my life when I have felt like the proverbial sailor left adrift at sea following a shipwreck. I went to college knowing that I either wanted to be a major league baseball player or president of the United States. I discovered once I got there that politics and government was my calling, and I experienced a period of rapid advancement and success in that pursuit. I had benchmarked the careers of Presidents Kennedy, Nixon and Johnson. Each elected to Congress at age 30. Nixon and Johnson from the two largest states in the union. I ran at age 29, got elected and during my two terms received a number of recognitions by Time Magazine (200 Emerging Young Leaders), New Times Magazine (one of 10 Most Effective Members of Congress), Texas Monthly (Top Five Texas Congressmen) and the Dallas Times Herald ("one of best ever sent to Congress from Texas"). Being from Texas, the second largest state, and with the recognition I was receiving, would provide the ideal launching pad for my goal, I felt.

All the building blocks were falling into place, and then the shipwreck -- a failed race for the U.S. Senate in Texas after my second term. Kennedy, Johnson and Nixon had each taken this exact step and I calculated that this would also be my next step. At age 34, with a wife and four children, I was now out of a job and my rapid ascent toward my life goal had now crashed and burned. Part of the heartbreak was having to part ways with my Congressional staff of 25. We were all young, very close, idealistic and driven for the larger cause. I had to clear out my office in the Cannon House Office Building by January 1. I went in on a day between Christmas and New Year's. I was there alone and cried. I've cried at funerals, of course, but, rarely for other reasons. This was a hard, hard day for me. For a year as I weighed options for this next stage of my life, I was truly adrift and aimless for the first time in my life.

The second "shipwreck" came fifteen years later after I had found my second calling with Alexander Proudfoot Company, a global management consulting company. After deploying to Singapore and serving as President of the Asia-Pacific region for eight years, I had returned and become President and COO worldwide and was the CEO-designate. We were a public company, traded on the London Stock Exchange and had a board chairman at the time, who had become embroiled in a financial scandal at the company where he was the full-time CEO. Even though the scandal had nothing to do with us, every time his name was mentioned in association with the scandal in news articles, the article would also mention that he was non-executive chairman of our company. Our share price fell, over a six-month period by 75%. I decided with the support of the executive team that it was time to take action to oust him as board chairman. I wrote a letter to the board making what I felt was a compelling case for his ouster given the negative publicity we were getting and the share price drop. To shorten a longer story, the board consisting largely of his selected members voted 5-4 to keep him. One would think that someone with my background in politics, would have known how to count votes better. Understandably, now emboldened, he fired me. I was now adrift again and was for about a nine-month period until I was recruited to join another consulting firm. About a year later, he was finally ousted, and after a ten-year hiatus, I was recruited to return to Proudfoot and worked another fifteen years, retiring as Vice-Chairman.

My purpose and calling in this third career is to articulate and share a message of hope and a practical recipe for those who are dealing with the unprecedented levels of stress and anxiety, and having difficulty coping without the use of self-medication, often with health destroying substances. All the steps outlined in this chapter are available to each of us.

Purpose is the roof of the Brick House. During my life, even though, I didn't know about the Six Pillars, as such, I have largely followed a similar regimen. Seven to eight hours of sleep, eating nutritional food (too much sometimes), exercised, had a wide circle of friends, and appreciated the healing properties of nature. Yoga and meditation, which I consider to be very effective in helping to sedate the monkey are additions within the past twelve years. What I have learned is that even with the other pillars, a life without some defining purpose is incomplete and can add significantly to our stress and anxiety levels. As said before, it can be large and public, or it can be more modest and out of the public eye, but it provides direction and gives the other pillars what is needed to ensure both the physical, mental, and emotional benefits that ensure a longer and more productive lifespan.

Pillar One:
Sleep--the Foundation

Sleep is the foundation upon which a life of balance and equilibrium rests. It is the foundation upon which the other pillars rest. No matter how physically fit, how well one eats the proper diet, exercises, or performs on the other pillars of well-being, sleep deprivation can negate the rest.

Not getting enough sleep has a number of both short and long-term debilitating effects on both our mental and physical health. Low stress situations can trigger emotional responses far out of proportion to their intent. Insufficient sleep has also been linked to aggression, including exaggerated fear and anxiety.

> *"The balm of hurt minds...sleep the chief nourisher in life's feast... sleep that knits up the raveled sleeve of care*
>
> *—MacBeth*

We are a sleep-deprived nation as is most of the developed world, including Western Europe, U.K., South Korea, and Japan. The common denominator among these countries is the incessant drive to succeed that can be the dark side of free-market economies.

In addition to body fatigue, there is growing evidence that disrupted or insufficient sleep can have widespread damaging effects on both physical and mental health. Heart disease, high blood pressure, stroke and Type 2 diabetes are all exacerbated by sleep deprivation. Brain fog, otherwise defined by muddled thinking, less energy, increased irritability and dampened sex drive are all by-products of less than the necessary seven to eight hours

For example, a major study suggests that middle-aged people who are chronically short on shut-eye face an increased risk of developing dementia in their later years. The study, published last spring in the journal Nature Communications, followed nearly 8,000 50-year-olds in Britain for about 25 years. Compared with those who averaged seven hours of sleep a night, the study participants who slept six hours or less on weeknights were 30 percent more likely to be diagnosed with dementia nearly three decades later.

The Centers for Disease Control and Prevention recommends between 7 and 9 hours of sleep each night for adults, and many Americans are getting 4-5 hours, some due to a belief that top performers need to work more and sleep and rest less. Others just have trouble sleeping due to the random wanderings of the "monkey", who is no respecter of the need for sleep and rest. The consequences are several and debilitating.

- Anxiety: The pace of life in the digital age along with the 24/7 news cycle are enough by themselves to create the unprecedented level of anxiety that bedevils many, if not most of us. Add sleep deprivation to this and it can become toxic and appears to be a major contributing factor in the soaring suicide rate among teens. A recent California study including over 100 teen suicides found 100% were sleep deprived. It should be added that there were other factors at play, as well, including peer pressure from over consumption of social media, school angst brought on by the pressure of making grades and good test scores in order to get into the right schools, etc. These pressures are difficult enough to manage without all the consequences that arise from loss of sleep.
- Anger: Mood swings are prevalent among the sleep deprived with a tendency to "fly off the handle" and react emotionally to events that otherwise would be seen as inconsequential. The

Journal of Experimental Psychology in a recent study involving two different control groups found that those getting 4 ½ hours of sleep reported much greater amounts of anger and distress than the other group which had averaged 7 ½ hours per night.

— Impatience: Damage to family relations and the work environment, including relationship destroying verbal abuse are often the consequence. Impatience is linked inextricably to anger and the inability to experience instant success on whatever the task at hand may be. Professor Jeanne Duffy at the Harvard Medical School puts it succinctly, "it makes us short-tempered" and the unintended consequences are often quite dramatic.

— Reckless risk-taking: Carefully considered risk-taking is a feature of success in life. Yet, much of the behavior that we look back on and say, "that was stupid, why did I do that", can be traced to anxiety, anger, and impatience often aided and abetted by some form of self-medication (alcohol or otherwise).

A groundbreaking new study by the Center for Human Sleep Science at UC Berkeley demonstrates the self-medication benefits, connecting sleep to anxiety relief on a neural level. The study's authors believe their findings designate sleep as a natural, non-pharmaceutical alternative for anxiety disorder treatment. "Our study strongly suggests that insufficient sleep amplifies levels of anxiety and, conversely, that deep sleep helps reduce such stress," says study lead author Eti Ben Simon, a postdoctoral fellow in the Center for Human Sleep Science at UC Berkeley. Brain scans after the sleepless night revealed that the participants' medial prefrontal cortex had shut down. This structure usually helps regulate anxiety. Meanwhile, the same brain scans also revealed that participants' deeper emotional centers were overactive after not sleeping.

"People with anxiety disorders routinely report having disturbed sleep, but rarely is sleep improvement considered as a clinical recommendation for lowering anxiety," Simon says. "Our study not only establishes a causal connection between sleep and anxiety, but it identifies the kind of deep NREM sleep we need to calm the overanxious brain."

"The findings suggest that the decimation of sleep throughout most industrialized nations and the marked escalation in anxiety disorders in these same countries is perhaps not coincidental, but causally related," "The best bridge between despair and hope is a good night of sleep."

What To Do About It

Most of us, understand the need for more sleep and don't need a lot of evangelizing on the topic. The bigger question, and its one most all of us have struggled with at various times during our lives. There are a number of practical steps we can take to improve on both the amount and the quality of our sleep.

- Maintaining a consistent sleep schedule and wind-down regimen
- Avoid all sources of caffeine in the late afternoon and evening, as well as a big heavy meal close to bedtime.
- A cool, dark, and quiet bedroom
- Avoiding the glare of screens after dark (or using blue light blocking glasses if you must work late)
- Meditation and journaling
- Avoiding heavy foods before bed (a protein shake or a handful almonds is a good snack)
- An Epsom salt warm bath
- White-noise machine
- Melatonin

I personally follow each of these, except for avoiding the glare of screens after dark. Some elaboration on Melatonin is probably worthwhile. I first heard of it twenty years ago, when I was flying to both Europe and Asia and dealing with jetlag. I found it very effective and have continued it ever since, long after jetlag was no longer a part of my life. I use a 5mg or 10mg chewable gummy taken about an hour before bedtime and before the warm bath. Please below for recommended dosage for those just starting. Body size and other issues that vary from person to person effect the dosage amount. It is not addictive, and is available in liquid, gummy or tablet form.

It is a natural brain chemical that we're all born with and that depletes as we age. It is a hormone that our brains naturally produce. Most will find it a very effective and important addition to your sleep regimen. There are other cases that may require medical diagnosis and treatment, such as sleep apnea, restless legs syndrome or mood disorders like depression.

How does melatonin work?

During the day, the brain's pea-sized pineal gland remains inactive. A few hours before our natural sleep time, as it starts to get dark outside and the light entering our retina fades, the gland switches on to flood the brain with melatonin. As levels of melatonin rise, levels of cortisol, the stress hormone, fall. Respiration slows. Soon, our eyelids begin to droop.

Instead of a lights-out trigger, melatonin acts more like a dimmer switch, turning the day functions off and switching night functions on. So, taking a melatonin supplement is sort of like taking a dose of sunset, tricking your body into feeling like it's nighttime. It doesn't put you to sleep as much as it tells the body that it's time to sleep.

What about dosage

Many experts recommend starting with the smallest available dosage — 0.5 milligrams to 1 milligram, 30 minutes to an hour before bedtime — and seeing how you do from there. If that has no effect, the dose can be gradually increased. I started with 3 mg and through trial and error over the years have varied between 5 and 10mgs. Feeling groggy or hung over is a sign that the dose is probably too high.

All of the remedies are logical and well understood, although not practiced by many. Since the purpose of this entire book is to equip one with practices that provide natural and self-medication, some may not understand the inclusion of, it, as a supplement to take as an enhancement to the other practices.

Taking a melatonin supplement before bed will not affect the pineal gland's natural secretion of it. However, there are many factors that can decrease its production over time. Aging plays the biggest role in natural reduction of melatonin production. Stress, and smoking also contribute to a decrease in production.

This is sleep, the first pillar in managing the monkey.

Pillar Two: Nutrition: Stop Eating Like an American

That statement of "stop eating like an American" is pretty jarring, yet America is now second only to Mexico in obesity. America is a land of plenty and the "shining city on the hill" reference is at the center of the concept of American Exceptionalism. Food and large portions of food have become intertwined with this idea of we have plenty and we will eat plenty.

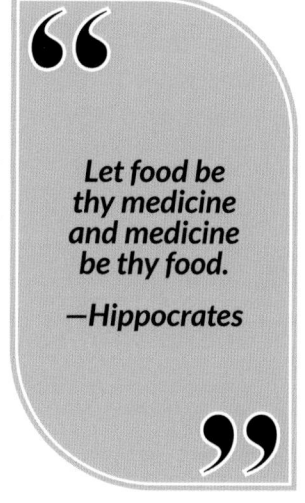

Let food be thy medicine and medicine be thy food.

—Hippocrates

It is an eye-opener to travel to other parts of the world and return and suddenly notice the difference in obesity in America compared to other parts of the world. The Mediterranean diet referenced later in this chapter, as the name implies, refers to those countries that either border the Mediterranean Sea or are located in near proximity to it. Travel to these countries, like France, Italy, Spain, Portugal are all good examples of the "eye-opener experience" mentioned above.

Many restaurants in America, particularly fast-food outlets, market the size of their meals, even above the taste and quality. Several countries in Asia have noticed a marked increase in the weight gains after American fast-food chains came to their shores.

The media-age has created an obsession with weight, based mostly on physical appearance and the desire to have a good physical appearance. An even more important and compelling reason is the impact on our physical and mental health.

Emotional eating is one way employed by many to self-medicate the stress and anxiety in their lives. Obesity can be just as much a killer as alcohol and opioids. In addition to diabetes, hypertension, and cardiovascular disease, the type of food and amounts of food that we eat are a leading cause of cancer. A recent study published in the JNCI Cancer Spectrum said that a low intake of vegetables, fruits, whole grains and dairy products along with a high intake of processed meats, red meats and sugary beverages were major contributing factors to the uptick in cancer rates.

Men 45 to 64 years old and ethnic minorities, including blacks and Hispanics had the highest rates compared with the other groups. The pace of life and the overall perceived need for convenience drives many to fast food and processed food with the unintended consequence of health destroying habits developed and reinforced over time.

Recent studies show that depression can be both caused by diet and can be treated by making different food choices. Nutritional psychiatry, a new field is an outgrowth of this and among this newly emerging field is a finding by researchers from Rush University that depression among elderly adults is less likely to develop with a change to a more nutritious diet. Depression can be genetic or caused by traumatic events in life, but at its root is an unhealthy brain and there is strong and compelling evidence that healthy eating can have a dramatic positive impact on mental health.

The term "gut-brain axis" is a term most of us aren't familiar with, nor are most aware of the impact of that what we eat has on our mental health. In simple and summary terms, a happy gut ensures a happy us.

Too often, when mired in a bad mood, many of us will "eat something" to feel better. This is emotional eating and is a major contributing factor to the obesity epidemic. Many who aren't self-medicating with alcohol or pills will reach for a salty or sugary snack, or for a full sit-down large portion "comfort food" meal. As I mentioned in an earlier chapter, I was guilty of this for many years. I've always been "physically fit" as measured by most of the traditional metrics (cholesterol, blood pressure, heart rate, triglycerides, etc.), even while being overweight. Not understanding the importance of gut-health, I always felt I could "run it off", and this worked for a long time, until my metabolism "retired", as it does for most in the mid-40s.

Most are more likely to blame a bad mental health day on stressful life events, poor sleep, and stress in general, than diet, since most have never made the connection. Not enough have thought about the need for an integrated, holistic regimen that includes, not only sleep, and exercise, but also the need for more attention to the food we eat, the need for a mindfulness practice in our lives, more focus on social interaction, and interacting with nature more.

Most of us will focus on sleep, which is the foundation for mental balance and equilibrium So far, the results of those efforts appear to be mixed; 45% of respondents said they frequently struggle with issues of mental illness, while another one in ten only feel like they're in an actively good mood for one day out of the week.

Serotonin, the hormone that influences mood and feelings of happiness, is regulated by the gut -- our second brain. When the microbiome of the digestive system is optimized, all the body's systems work better — including the brain."

As discussed in Chapter Three and the section featuring Dr. Kara Fitzgerald's book, Younger You what we eat has a very significant impact on how we age. A sustained change from a typical to an optimized diet from early age could translate into an increase in life expectancy of more than 10 years," claim the Norwegian authors of a scientific study published in the open-ended journal PLOS (formerly the Public Library of Science)

"Our results indicate that for individuals with a typical Western diet, sustained dietary changes at any age may give substantial health benefits, although the gains are the largest if changes start early in life," the researchers assert. "An optimal diet had substantially higher intake than a typical diet of whole grains, legumes, fish, fruits, vegetables, and included a handful of nuts, while reducing red and processed meats, sugar-sweetened beverages, and refined grains."

However, the study finds that altering your diet by your 20s has increased benefits than changing it later in life. The researchers claim that 20-year-old males who adopt a healthier diet extend their life 13 years. Females who better their eating choices can add 10.7 years.

There are still benefits of changing your eating habits at older ages, but they are not as pronounced, according to the research. Focusing on a healthier diet could also lengthen the lives of older adults, the study said. By starting at age 60, a woman could still increase her lifespan by eight years. Men starting a healthier diet at age 60 might add nearly nine years to their lives. For those who are 80 years old who practice a healthier diet could gain approximately three years.

Dr. David Katz, a specialist in preventive and lifestyle medicine and nutrition, says: "The notion that improving diet quality would reduce the risk of chronic disease and premature death is long established, and it only stands to reason that less chronic disease and premature death means more life expectancy."

Diets Are Often Roundtrips

Most weight loss regimens work if we stick with them and mobilize the discipline over time to stick with them. Too often, once the goal is reached, especially if we have been eating to medicate emotional imbalances in our lives, the pounds return. Even the word diet subconsciously communicates deprivation. Research shows that food restriction just makes you want to eat more. And over the long term, dieting can backfire, triggering your body's survival defenses, slowing your metabolism and making it even harder to lose weight in the future.

If a healthier mind and body is the goal, old ideas about counting calories, banning your favorite foods and measuring success by a number on a scale, need to be replaced with a new mind set of eating to be a whole-body *health regimen* not a *diet* with all the deprivation connotations that go with that.

So, what's the alternative? Many weight researchers are encouraging a new approach to healthy eating based on brain science. A variety of techniques that encourage mindful awareness of how we eat, acceptance related to the foods we want to eat, and intuitive eating exercises can be used to quell cravings and reshape our eating habits.

"The paradigms around willpower don't work," said Dr. Judson Brewer, an associate professor in behavioral and social sciences at the Brown University School of Public Health who has studied mindful eating practices. "You have to start by knowing how your mind works."

Why Restrictive Diets Are Often a Roundtrip

Dr. Traci Mann, in her book *Secrets From the Eating Lab,* who heads the health and eating laboratory at the University of Minnesota, notes that the weight often returns and restrictive eating can affect memory and executive function, leading to obsessive food thoughts and trigger a surge in cortisol, a stress hormone. "You might take it off in the short term, but it comes back. It happens no matter who you are; it happens to people with great willpower and to people with crappy willpower."

Mindful Eating

I have discovered, as a former emotional eater that the adoption or more mindfulness activities into my life, like yoga and meditation, aided and abetted by sleep and the other pillars, have caused my appetite for sugar and large portions to have largely disappeared. The "hunger", I have discovered, was a result of the cortisol triggered by the stress and anxiety of the high-pressure jobs I've had in both politics and business. It has been quite a revelation to observe the palpable difference in my appetite for certain foods and portions once I learned to deal with the stress and anxiety in my life through mindful eating.

Ice cream, Oreos, Peanut M&Ms all were my go-to of choice in hotel rooms around the world as I unwound from either a long flight or a stressful negotiation with a client. The brain learns to associate eating ice cream with feeling good. While there's nothing wrong with ice cream, it can become a problem when we start eating it unthinkingly after an emotional trigger, such as when we feel stressed or angry. I was totally oblivious to the connection between my emotional state and the triggers behind them leading to both my portion choices and my medication with sugar in the hotel room while watching television or reading.

Awareness, slowing down and thinking about what you're eating is mindfulness simply defined. Try not to focus on weight loss, food restriction or eliminating favorite foods from your diet. Avoid labeling foods as "good" or "bad." Your goal this week is to focus on the tastes and textures of food, and how you feel before, during and after eating. The monkey and the mind chatter will interrupt this, just as it does all other activities of your life. It will also take time to incorporate this into your life as a permanent new relationship with food. In Chapter Six, I suggest a sixty-six-day period of commitment on your part to make this new lifestyle a permanent part of your behavior.

Foods to Eat and to Avoid

A Mediterranean-style regimen, as referenced above is rich in micronutrients like magnesium, vitamin E and selenium that have anti-inflammatory effects, and its high-fiber content fosters lower levels of two potent inflammatory substances, IL-6 and TNF-alpha. It is a plant-based diet focused on fruits, like strawberries, blueberries, apples, grapes, oranges and cherries and vegetables, especially dark greens like kale, spinach and arugula. whole grains, and cold-water fish, Omega-3 fatty fish like salmon, mackerel, tuna and sardines and plants like soybeans and flax seeds that contain omega-3 fatty acids, and nuts like almonds and walnuts, and olive oil.

Dr. Frank Hu, professor of nutrition and epidemiology at the Harvard T.H. Chan School of Public Health, strongly recommends limiting or eliminating consumption of foods known to have a pro-inflammatory effect. These include all refined carbohydrates like white bread, white rice and pastries; sugar-sweetened beverages; deep-fried foods; and red meat and processed meats. They are the very same foods with well-established links to obesity (itself a risk factor for inflammation), heart disease and Type 2 diabetes.

Coffee and tea also contain protective polyphenols, among other anti-inflammatory compounds.

What To Do About It:

Mindful eating is the starting point. Dealing with the root cause of the food choices and the portion sizes are the important first step:

The Mediterranean-style regimen: fruits, vegetables, olive oil, yogurt, cheese, legumes, nuts, seafood, whole grains, and small portions of red meat. This provides the nutrition our brain needs, regulates inflammation and supports the good bacteria in our gut. (Dr. Lisa Mosconi, Brain Food: The Surprising Science of Eating for Cognitive Power)

The overwhelming consensus among nutritionists and health-experts is that the wisest course is a long-term, sustainable regimen that promotes and supports good mental and physical health. This is the second pillar in managing the monkey.

Pillar Three:
Movement/Exercise: Sitting Is the New Smoking!

"Sitting is the new smoking" is a popular phrase coined by Dr. James Levine, director of the Mayo Clinic at Arizona University in Phoenix, Arizona. This is probably a little hyperbolic but, certainly has some merit and is a good metaphor to bring attention to a big problem.

Mass migration from the countryside to the cities and suburbs is a hallmark of the post WWII period. One writer has called it the greatest migration in history. Less realized and reported on is the mass migration to the "inside", meaning to the chair and sofa and all the consequent negative consequences.

Throughout its history, America and its people have been "on the move" with jobs and professions that required physical labor and movement and play and recreation activities. This migration is one of the unintended consequences of the Digital Age, and the negative impact on the nations mental and physical health is palpable. As mentioned earlier, America is now second only to Mexico in obesity. Cardiovascular disease, type-2 diabetes, high blood pressure, higher cholesterol, liver damage are only a few of the negative impacts. Arthritis is made worse by a sedentary lifestyle.

Will Parkinson:
The Yellow Brick Road on One Leg

"I might not be here today, had I not reluctantly walked through that door and into my first yoga class." Almost 50 years following a traumatic, life-changing event, the enormous toll on body, mind and spirit had brought him to a breaking point.

A Tom Sawyer-like idyllic childhood in the Mississippi Delta, hunting, fishing and playing sports is brought to a traumatizing abrupt, life-changing halt at age 16 by a hunting accident. He loses his leg, after being accidentally shot by a close friend. Already haunted by the memory, as a four-year story, of watching a 12-year-old next door neighbor drown in front of the boat dock at the front of their house, he now begins his life adapting to life on one leg and the prosthetic that came with this life-altering event. The damage of such events to body, mind and spirit are incalculable.

Prosthetic technology in the 1970s was in its infancy and finding a fit that was comfortable was a major challenge. He describes the next 25 years as being so painful that he could often hardly walk.

He is now a successful businessman with five children and a life-partner and business partner in his wife Ashley. Yet, his lifetime search for freedom from the physical and emotional pain to this point is one marked by struggle and dependence on many of the crutches that so many default to in desperation to find some semblance of relief.

Hepatitis C Virus, diabetes, all came in succession over the years due both to his inability to exercise and the obesity that came from being an emotional eater. Medicating emotional pain with food can take as big a toll on physical health as alcohol and pills. "Eating was my drug." Finally, my prothesis was comfortable, but now my other leg was in constant pain due to the weight I was carrying. Neck pain, lower back pain and a broken wrist from a fall all came in succession requiring surgeries. "I was overweight, depressed, in constant pain and gaining more weight, then came a kidney stone, so large, I couldn't pass it without surgery. The medication for high cholesterol I was on was preventing me from sleeping. Additionally, he had been prescribed Interferon. This is usually prescribed to cancer patients for a six-week period. His treatment lasted for fifty weeks. "To say I was miserable is an understatement. I had the lingering effects of brain fog and memory loss for a long period of time afterward." He described his bedside table as looking like a Walgreens Pharmacy.

In desperation, my wife finally recommended I see a pain therapist. Having suffered from chronic pain herself, she said she had finally found relief in yoga and meditation. Being a hunter, fisherman and sports aficionado, I thought this was a ridiculous prescription, so I continued my self-destructive ways. After another two years of more pain, more medication and more weight-gain, Ashley finally persuaded me to go a class at LA Fitness. I looked through that glass-door, saw a lot of people sitting there on their mats waiting for class to start, and none looked remotely like me. I was getting ready to walk away, when this man, closer to my age, got up from his mat, walked all the way across the studio, and asked us to please come in. I will never forget him saying, "If you can breathe, you can do this." (Author full disclosure. That was the author of this book)

I felt the effects after the first session and two weeks later, I felt better than I had in 30 years. I was soon off the cholesterol and blood pressure medication. My craving for fried foods, gravy, French-fries, and sugar was all of sudden gone. "I don't like to use the work "miracle" too often, but the change in my life, physically, mentally, and spiritually, has been nothing short of that"

Those who have experienced the endorphin high from a vigorous cardiovascular workout, already appreciate the mind-body connection and the therapeutic mental effects of exercise. In her new book "52 Ways to Walk: The Surprising Science of Walking for Wellness and Joy, One Week at a Time," Annabel Streets says, "Movement is medicine. A 12-minute walk, for example alters 522 metabolites in our blood—molecules that affect the beating of our heart, the breath in our lungs, the neurons in our brain," she writes in the book out next month. "Oxygen rushes through us, affecting…our memory, creativity, mood, our capacity to think."

Dr. Ellen Vora, a psychiatrist. In her new book "The Anatomy of Anxiety: Understanding and Overcoming the Body's Fear Response," argues that physical activity is ignored by experts who are too focused on mental health from the neck up. "It's the low-hanging fruit," she says. "Brain chemistry, thoughts, behaviors might take years to address on the couch."

Physical activity changes levels of brain chemicals related to mood, such as dopamine and serotonin, and reduces inflammation throughout the body and brain, contributing physiologically to stouter mental health

High intensity exercise is the choice for many, especially the young. HIIT (high intensity interval training) is going all out on a particular exercise, like a treadmill or elliptical machine for a short burst of time, like 2-3 minutes to be followed a similar amount of time at a slower pace.

At the same time, though, a wealth of other studies this decade underscored that gentle exercise is also meaningful, even if it barely qualifies as exercise. A recent study found that older women who regularly strolled about two miles a day, or a little more than 4,000 steps, lived longer than women who covered only about 2,000 steps, or a mile. Going that lone extra mile altered how long and well women lived.

There has been a burst of research in the past two decades showing how exercise not only slows aging, but provides better brain functioning well into the senior years. In <u>various recent studies</u>, active older people's <u>muscles, immune systems</u>, blood cells and <u>even skin</u> appeared biologically younger, at a molecular level, than those of sedentary people.

Movement, of almost any kind and amount, has a significant effect on how we think and feel.

Physically active people are much less likely to develop depression or anxiety than sedentary people, no matter what types of activities they chose.

Walking, jogging, gardening, weight training, swimming, biking, hiking or even rising from an office or living room chair often and strolling across the room has been shown to trigger the endorphin chemical and make people less prone to mood problems than remaining still.

There are 109 chemicals and 22,000 genes in our bodies. These interior ecosystems and maintaining eco-balance, a process called *homeostasis* is critical to both our physical and mental health. The balance differs in fundamental ways between those who exercise and those who don't. People who exercise harbor different types and amounts of proteins in their bloodstreams, for instance, even if they have not been working out recently, and these patterns of proteins may play a role in reducing risks for metabolic problems such as diabetes or heart disease.

Exercisers' muscles also produce and release various vesicles, or tiny bubbles of cellular material, that carry biochemical messages from one tissue to another, recent research shows. The vesicles are not found to the same extent in the bloodstreams of the sedentary. Such microscopic messages between muscles and other tissues may be jump-starting biochemical processes that improve health.

Much is known by virtually everyone on the movement or exercise options available to all of us. I have been a diligent exerciser my entire life, particularly with running and weight training. I added yoga to the regimen about twelve years ago. The impact yoga has had on my ability to sedate the monkey and all the benefits that go with that has been palpable. I can't prove that it has had the most important impact on my DNA age being almost ten years younger (Chapter Three), but I believe the *homeostasis* impact of moving all the body chemicals around and back to their proper place is among the most important reasons and yoga and Pilates both do this. These 109 chemicals, all critical to keeping all the organs healthy and performing their proper function, are in the right place at birth and during our younger years, but get displaced as we age and especially as our lifestyle choices (diet, exercise) become more problematic

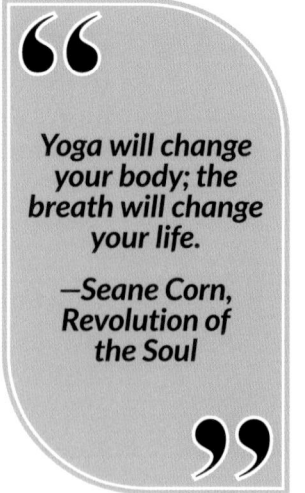

Yoga will change your body; the breath will change your life.

—Seane Corn, Revolution of the Soul

"Breathing is everything, it's absolutely everything. When we get overwhelmed, when our nervous system gets deregulated, one of the first things that we do is hold our breath. We de-oxygenate our system, and that makes our nervous system spike even more. And that spike, again, takes us out of the present mind. It closes off the rational part of our brain and it stimulates the primal or reptilian part of our brain. And therefore, we are reactive. When we breathe and take in that nutrient-rich oxygen into our body, it has an impact on the whole of our systems, helping our nervous system go from this, which is spiked or an activated nervous system, to a regulated nervous system. When our nervous system is regulated, I can hear differently. I can respond rather than react. It lets me be in present time, able to discern." (Seane Corn, Revolution of the Soul),

What to do about it: Walking, running, cycling, hiking, Pilates, yoga, tai chi, weight training, chair yoga

Pillar Four:
Meditation/Mindfulness: Be Here Now

The monkey lives only in the past or the future. There's no oxygen for him in the present moment

Over 80% of top business leaders meditate, according to author Tim Ferriss who has interviewed over 200 world-class performers. It has also become widely used in other high-stress professions, including Wall Street, professional sports, the military, first-responders, et al. It has been described as a warm bath for the mind. One prominent example, who has created enormous personal financial wealth and "wellth" is billionaire

Ray Dalio, the 72-year-old billionaire, twice a day, closes his eyes and repeats a short mantra in his head for 20 minutes at a time. It's a practice he says he adopted in 1969 — six years before he founded Westport, Connecticut-based hedge fund Bridgewater Associates. Over the following five decades, Dalio built Bridgewater into the world's largest hedge fund before stepping down as co-CEO in 2017. Today, Bridgewater manages more than $150 billion in assets.

Since stepping down, Dalio says he's been on a mission to widely share the knowledge that helped enable his success. That includes his meditation practice, which he once called "the single most important reason for whatever success I've had.

R.A.I.N.

It has been long determined, that "what we resist persists." Most often our first reaction to fear and anxiety is to feel embarrassed, weak, inadequate push back and try to move on from it. We quickly learn that it won't just go away, it stays, and the monkey keeps talking. Thoughts create body sensations. Fearful or anxious thoughts create stomach knots, clenched jaws, tight shoulders, etc.

For as long as I can remember, I have awakened, even after a good night's sleep with a racing mind, and it's never thoughts about all the abundance in my life, it's about whatever I'm feeling fearful of or threatened by at the time. A few years ago, I learned about how important a contribution that including a daily practice of meditation could be to my overall physical and mental health. There are countless meditation techniques and practices and for variety's sake, I use many of them. For these morning episodes, I have learned to use a technique, RAIN, popularized by Tara Brach, a prominent and psychologist and author. She is the founder of the Insight Meditation Community in Washington, D. C.

RAIN is an acronym for *recognize, accept, investigate and nurture.* I encourage the reader to google her and RAIN. There are a number of guided sessions on her website that one can use. In summary, instead of pushing back and resisting, recognizing the body sensation, the thought/s creating it, accepting that here it is again and I'm very familiar with it, since it visits a lot of the time are the important two first steps. Investigating the thought and how real and large is the threat, REALLY?

Often this investigation or analysis will reveal that it's some thought whose source is from some long-ago event or experience that became hardwired into our mind and has remained since.

In my case, the financial struggles from childhood that I remember of my parents and their struggles to provide for our family have given me a lifelong subliminal emotion of deprivation and fear of having to revisit that experience. No matter, my current state of financial security, and how getting out of bed, seeing the daylight, getting dressed and out to start the day makes it all seem so trivial and non-threatening, the awakening experience remains the same.

Nurturing through mindful breathing and concentrating on the affected body part, usually a modest knot in the stomach and getting into a state of "being here now" usually brings back to a state of feeling non-threatened and seeing that the perceived threat isn't real after all. This is RAIN and I highly recommend that you investigate it for possible use in your own life.

The Basics

Finding a comfortable, preferable dark and quiet place sitting, lying down or on a meditation cushion.

Setting aside time for formal meditation is an important way to establish a routine and get comfortable with the practice. Even just a few minutes a day can make a big difference.

But we shouldn't stop being mindful when we stop meditating. "The purpose of mindfulness meditation is to become mindful throughout all parts of our life, so that we're awake, present and openhearted in everything we do," said Tara Brach "Not just when we're sitting on the cushion."

Mindfulness meditation isn't about letting your thoughts wander. But it isn't about trying to empty your mind, either. Instead, the practice involves paying close attention to the present moment — especially our own thoughts, emotions and sensations — whatever it is that's happening.

Basic Mindfulness Meditation

You can practice mindfulness meditation on your own anytime and anywhere. But listening to basic guided meditations can also be helpful, especially when getting started. Instructions from an experienced teacher can help remind us to come back to the present moment, let go of distracting thoughts and not be so hard on ourselves. There are apps like Insight Timer, my favorite for both volume and variety of different techniques. Calm and Ten-Percent Happier are two other good options.

You may be wondering, how you can breathe any differently than you already do? Most of us react to stress by shallow breathing. Simply defined, mindful breathing is inhaling deeply through the nose, up from your diaphragm, pausing at the top for three to four seconds, and exhaling through the nose, all the way to the bottom, and pausing again at the bottom. Repeating this rhythmic process while participating in a yoga session, or as part of a 20-minute meditation session practiced on a consistent basis, is the true path to "peace of mind." (See the next pages for several techniques.)

Getting to "now" and remaining in the now standard time (NST) zone requires managing a consistent rhythm in your breathing. Most of us breathe from the chest, and the shallow breath signals to the brain that we are stressed. How often do you say or think, "I just want to be happy!" The state of "happiness"—a mind free of anxiety, worry, and stress—is one we pursue throughout our lives. The secret to this, one can find, like the Scarecrow, the Tin Man, and the Cowardly Lion, lies within. Furthermore, it is readily accessible through life's greatest gift—the breath, the Yellow Brick Road. Stay on it... the Emerald City is very near. Just as Dorothy was cautioned about the hostile territory through which she would have to walk, you as a rhythmic breather will also find distractions in the form of "mind chatter" that will challenge your ability to stay on the path. Our thoughts, emotions, and fears are constant topics of silent conversation in our minds, and a constant barrier to mind peace. Like everything else, "managing the monkey" becomes much easier through following a disciplined practice

Learn how to pay close attention to the present moment with this meditation exercise with these five examples:

--Body Scan: Start at the top of your head. Slowly and deliberately, bring your attention to the surface of your skin, one inch at a time. See if you can feel your scalp, your ears, your eyelids and your nose. Continue in this manner, moving across the face, over the ears, down the neck and shoulders and all the way down to your toes.

At first, it might seem as if you don't feel anything at all. But as you progress, you might begin to notice a whole world of new sensations. Some of the feelings might be pleasant, a gentle warmth, a comfortable weight. Some feelings might be neutral — tingling or itching. And some might be unpleasant. Your feet might feel soreness somewhere.

Whatever the sensation is, just note it. If you need to move to relieve real pain, do so. But try not to react — labeling the experience good or bad — even if it's unpleasant. Instead, just acknowledge what it is you're feeling, and continue with the body scan. And of course, if you realize your mind has wandered, simply note the thought, and return your attention to the body

- Darth Vader Breath: also, called ocean breath. I find this technique the most effective, and there are several ways of doing it. My preferred way is to curl my tongue up to the roof of the mouth, inhale through the nose, up deeply from the pelvic floor, up through the diaphragm, pausing three to four seconds at the top, visualize a small hole in the throat, and exhale slowly, but resolutely, making the Darth Vader noise or ocean sound out the imagined hole in the throat.
- Taco: This technique is especially effective in cooling the body and brain after a vigorous, sweaty workout or power yoga session. Curl the tongue, like a taco, and inhale deeply through the mouth, holding for a count of two to three seconds and then exhale through the nose.
- Alternate Nostril Method: This technique is better utilized as part of a meditation session or at the opening of a yoga session, as it requires using the hands to manipulate the nostrils alternately, and this is difficult during an active yoga session as the arms and hands are very active during a standard session.
- Left Nostril Breathing: Find a comfortable seated position. Block your right nostril with right index finger, close your eyes, relax your jaw and brow, inhale deeply and long, pause at the top for three to four seconds, then exhale long and slowly through the left nostril. On the inhale, you might add silently the word "letting" and on the exhale, "go." Continue for three to five minutes.
- Bellows Breath: This technique is particularly effective for "jump-starting" a yoga session, as it is a quick energizer, consisting of deep inhales, followed by fast, vigorous exhales. A set of three of these, followed by reverting to the Darth Vader method, is good for mid-afternoon or after-work sessions, when energy may be lagging. The challenge to "breathe mindfully" becomes an even bigger challenge when you try to synchronize your breathing with a consistent set of yoga poses

as you go through a session. Don't fret over the "wandering" but just gently acknowledge the thought and come back to your breath. You will find the effort and patience worth the time invested.

When the Mind Wanders….and it will

It's inevitable: During meditation, your mind will roam. You may notice other sensations in the body, things happening around you, or just get lost in thought, daydreaming about the past or present, possibly judging yourself or others. There's nothing wrong with this — thinking is just as natural as breathing. "It's the natural conditioning of the mind to wander," said Ms. Brach.

You don't need to pull your attention right back to the breath. Instead, let go of whatever it was you were thinking about, reopen your attention, then gently return your awareness to the breath, being present for each inhalation and exhalation.

After a few breaths, invariably, the mind will wander again. Don't beat yourself up about this. It's natural. What's important is how we respond when it happens. Simply acknowledge whatever it is you were thinking of — without ascribing too much judgment to it, without letting it carry you away — and take a moment to come back to the present, and resume your meditation

Faranaha Surya Namaskar: The Tin Man/ Heartbreak, Trauma and Cancer

In the Wizard of Oz, the Tin Man yearned for a new heart in order to be in love again.

Miranda Lambert won the song of the year on the American Country Music Award Show saying, "Hey there Mr. Tin Man, you don't know how lucky you are. I've been on the road you're on and it didn't get me very far. You ain't missing nothing because love is so damn hard. Take it from me darling, you don't want a heart. Hey there mister Tin Man I'm so glad we talked this out. You can take mine if you want it. It's in pieces now By the way, if you don't mind the scars, you give me your armor and you can have my heart."

These lyrics have a particular resonance for Farahana Surya Namaskar, divorced and a single mother of a 10-year-old son. She went through a painful divorce after seven years of marriage. Already traumatized by childhood traumas that include growing up in an abusive home environment and sexual assault at the age of ten by a male teacher, she discovered that her way to begin healing was to begin an inward journey through meditation to discover herself and what she needed to navigate the choppy seas in her life.

While in the process of healing and coming to terms with the damage to her psyche and self-image a third tsunami, breast cancer appears and is diagnosed. "There is a book titled, *The Body Keeps Score"*, she says. When asked if the emotionally undigested stress and anxiety from childhood trauma and divorce were primary contributing factors to the cancer diagnosis, she answered "absolutely." The adage, "We can't change the external events in our lives, but we can, through mindfulness meditation find a way to navigate the choppy seas better," was truly being tested in her life.

Amazingly through all of this drama, she was serving as a divorce coach to others, and leading mindfulness meditation classes. As a divorce coach she had to deal with the topic of love and heartbreak and all the personal trauma that goes with it. This is not an easy issue for someone to talk about especially when it involved their own life and the emotional wounds that are still fresh and somewhat raw,

She says that her biggest learning from her life journey so far is that allowing your mind to put you in victim mode is not a healthy way to live or deal with trauma, no matter the damage. After going through the first reaction that we all have, of "Why me, what did I do to deserve all of this, feeling guilt and shame from both the divorce and the trauma from years ago, she discovered journaling and meditation as the best avenues for both healing and self-discovery. Regarding the divorce, accepting that it "takes two to tango" and that she may have also contributed to the breakup was a big first step.

"I use mindfulness as my mirror, and I reference a mirror because for me mindfulness helps me look at myself. It helps keep me accountable for the experiences I create in my life. I refuse to get into the mentality where I feel stuck or feel like I am the victim of my circumstance. I have been there before, it's a dark, hopeless and scary place to be. Trust me, even as I share this, none of this is easy, nor does it always flawlessly and naturally come to me. Real life experiences continue to challenge me like they do all of us. Being a single mom is by no means easy and challenges continue to unfold. But I know that I have to go through it all. I just have to continue to ask myself, what perspective am I going to respond with? Is life happening to me, or for me? If I fall back into my old narrative that life is happening to me, I will quickly fall into that dark hopeless victim state. If I remind myself again and again that life is in fact happening for me, I am once again gifting myself the opportunity to be open, to be curious and allow myself to trust and discover the magic and wonder that I truly believe life wishes to offer to of all of us.

The truth is, I cannot change the events of my past, but I can change my *perception* of the past. Perception is simply the state of my mind, the story and narrative I want to create and tell. I want the story I tell about the past to be that my past did not break me, it is what built me to be who I am today and what I continue to aspire to be. The past introduced me to the most courageous parts of me and showed me the capacity of my resilience which I had never known before. My past has taught me to reject complacency, to challenge myself in ways so that I can grow and become a better version of myself. My past taught me not to settle for mediocre, and to take accountability for my choices and the quality of my life.

We cannot put the onus on somebody else to love us the way we wish to be loved without loving ourselves that way. The past seven years has really taught me to recognize that everything that we are seeking outside of ourselves actually exists within us. We are not separate from that which we desire. We have just been looking for it all in the wrong place. It is not out there somewhere in the world, it is right here, right within us. Simply going inward will reveal that which we are seeking."

The initial prognosis and medical advice were to get a double mastectomy. She decided against breast removal, had the cancerous tissue removed and is now, thankfully now cancer-free. "While I have made it through all of this, she says, and developed more resilience, I haven't devoted enough time and effort to self-care as I should have and need to. That's my new determination going forward."

Mindfulness and sleep

Inasmuch as sleep is the foundation for creating a life of balance and equilibrium, it is worthwhile to explore how mindfulness affects our sleep. As defined above, Mindfulness is a mental state, succinctly defined as "being here now" -- achieved by focusing our awareness on the present moment, optimally practiced as outlined in the RAIN method as calmly recognizing, acknowledging, and accepting all feelings, thoughts, and bodily sensations?

Mindfulness not only improves the quality of our waking hours, but also improves our sleep habits and overall sleep hygiene. By being mindful and adding tailored practices into your daily routine, you can get better sleep and promote a more balanced lifestyle.

4 Ways Mindfulness Can Improve Your Sleep

-- Stress reduction

Life in the digital age has created an unprecedented level of stress and anxiety for all of us. The 24/7 news cycle, divisive political discourse, social media, over-scheduled days and endless to-do lists, make it nearly impossible to avoid the stress that comes with life today. By stepping back from a stressful situation and observing our thoughts and emotions more clearly, we are able to assess the true threat posed by whatever the thoughts are about. Most often, we discover the threat isn't real at all, or is vastly magnified by the monkey. A body-scan meditation session is a very effective option, I have found to reduce the anxious body sensations that are inhibiting my ability to go to sleep.

-- Mindfulness Can Help Decrease Sleeplessness

Particularly for those who struggle with falling asleep at night, bedtime comes hand in hand with sleeplessness. And, when we are greeted by sleeplessness frequently, we tend to enter a relentless cycle: we can't sleep, so we worry about not being able to sleep, which in turn keeps us from sleeping, and so on and so forth…

So, before jumping into your Mattress Firm mattress at night, try practicing mindfulness and meditation for sleep to keep from getting restless and sending yourself into a spiral of overwhelming thoughts. Instead of wreaking havoc on your sleep, seek to control your emotions and keep your thoughts at bay by putting into practice a few relaxation techniques for sleep every night.

-- Mindfulness Helps Lower Cortisol Levels

In add addition to reducing overall stress, recent studies have identified links between mindfulness practices and changes in cortisol levels, which in turn have helped improve sleep quality. Cortisol is a hormone that stimulates alertness and is important to the regulation of the body's 24-hour sleep-wake cycle. So, managing our cortisol levels allows us to maintain our body's natural cycle and get the proper sleep we need to function at our best every day.

-- Mindfulness or pills for sleep disorders?

Melatonin, our natural brain sleep chemical, taken as a supplement, along with a meditation practice before bedtime can lead to significant sleep gains, including reductions in total wake times. In addition to reducing insomnia, mindfulness can improve sleep quality, increase sleep times and cause better sleep efficiency. Since tomorrow's schedule and to-do list is often a persistent villain in sleep loss and particularly the waking at 3am syndrome, I keep my schedule and list in my phone on an app, revies and complete it about an hour ahead of bedtime, take my melatonin gummy, take the warm bath, and complete with a ten-fifteen-minute body scan meditation session. I almost always get a good, restful 7 hours and a 30–45-minute nap the next afternoon.

This is meditation/mindfulness the fourth pillar.

Pillar Five:
Friends and Social Networks: One is the loneliest number

How can the world grow smaller, more connected, more crowded, and yet more lonely for many? Dr. Heidi Grant Halvorson in an article for *Psychology Today* said, "loneliness is not the same as being a private person, or a 'loner'. Some need and enjoy more time with themselves. Loneliness is the difference between the amount of social interaction we have and the amount we want. It's about feeling isolated, the feeling of being an outcast."

At various times in our lives, we've all experienced the empty feeling of isolation, of being completely by ourselves. In the midst of a divorce or the death of a loved one, we can still feel alone and abandoned even with others around trying to console us and provide support.

Solitary confinement is one step removed from execution for a reason. It is the punishment for some of the most heinous crimes because it is considered to be a penalty even worse than death by many. Social isolation and loneliness are more lethal than smoking 15 cigarettes a day, or than obesity, according to research published by Julianne Holt-Lunstad of Brigham Young University. Since obesity is associated in the United States with 300,000 to 600,000 deaths a year, the implication is that loneliness is a huge, if silent, killer.

It is a pervasive problem on both ends of the age spectrum. The current generation, having grown up with video games, a range of electronic devices, and social media find making friends much more difficult than prior generations. My childhood, and the childhood of many was marked by playing outside with neighborhood children. There were enormous physical health benefits to this as well as developing the necessary social and emotional learning skills to successfully navigate relations with my peers and adults.

The National Academies of Sciences, Engineering and Medicine said has said that nearly one-quarter of Americans aged 65 and older who live in community settings have few relationships or infrequent social contact. It concluded that four decades of research have produced robust evidence that social isolation is associated with a significantly increased risk for early death from all causes

A common theme among seniors is the loss of a spouse, siblings or friends. It is not uncommon for a senior to resist mightily moving from their home to a retirement community. They often become disoriented and feel that life has become hopeless and purposeless.

Loneliness increases inflammation, heart disease, dementia and death rates, researchers say. It has become such a problem, a "loneliness epidemic", that it is now moving some government to organize initiatives to address it, like Great Britain which last year it appointed a minister for loneliness.

Surveys, by the AARP and others have recently shown that more than twenty percent of adults say that they often or always feel lonely. More than half of American adults are unmarried, and a quarter of Americans now live alone.

As said before, "stress is gasoline on the fire of aging." Stress hormones lead to inflammation and other health problems. Second, according to AARP research, people who are alone are less likely to go to doctor appointments, to take medicine or to exercise and eat a healthy diet. Professor Holt-Lunstad has found that greater social connection is associated with a 50 percent reduced risk of early death.

Many of those studying loneliness express a similar sense of mission about their research. Loneliness, says Louise Hawkley, a senior research scientist at the University of Chicago, "is a universal human experience, and being the social animals that we are, there must be implications when those social connections are not satisfied." There is a human need to be embedded, connected, integrated in a social network, she notes. When that social network is missing, "the consequences are very real in terms of mental and physical health."

The economic cost of loneliness

According to a study by researchers at the AARP Public Policy Institute and at Stanford and Harvard universities, the impacts of people living in social isolation add almost $7 billion a year to the cost of Medicare, mostly because of longer hospital stays — a result, researchers hypothesize, of not having community support at home. "Studies continue to show that the negative health effects of loneliness and isolation are especially harmful for older adults," says Lisa Marsh Ryerson, president of AARP Foundation. "Moreover, our own research has found that people with lower income are often at greater risk of isolation.."

Physical isolation, marital status, the number of close friends and family members, and the amount of television being watched, are all meaningful measures. "We need to define what exactly the issue is," says Julianne Holt-Lunstad, a professor of psychology and neuroscience at Brigham Young University. "Is it loneliness specifically, or is it people becoming more socially disconnected in a variety of ways?" Until recently, she adds, data on loneliness in and of itself was scarce. "But there are other kinds of indicators that are routinely collected that would suggest we are becoming less socially connected. We have evidence from census data that there has been an increase in the number of people who are living alone, and there are declining marriage rates and increasing rates of childlessness. We know that lacking social connection puts us at greater health risk."

The Lundstadt study and others acknowledge that some people who live alone by choice aren't necessarily lonely. It's also possible to feel disconnected, even within a tight-knit family or organization.

Holt-Lunstad is the coauthor of a set of 70 studies that followed a total of over 3 million participants over a seven-year period and came up with a startling conclusion. Those who live alone, those who describe themselves as very lonely and those who and those isolated from other people all faced roughly the same increased risk of an early death—32 percent for those living alone, 29 percent for those who were socially isolated from others and 26 percent for those who described themselves as very lonely.

"Certainly, physical and mental health issues can put you at risk for loneliness and isolation, but the evidence we have is independent of health status. Whether or not you are healthy, those who are more socially connected live longer."

The body has a long-term self-preservation mode and wants to approach others to survive, the lonely brain has a short-term self-defense mode and sees, erroneously, more foes than friends. In the lonely state, "the brain is misreading social signals that it should read normally; suddenly it doesn't have the correct translation. You put someone who is lonely into a room alone and every person who comes there will be perceived as a threat." Lonely people, Holt-Lundstadt continues, often misread a facial expression or tone of voice — characterizing curiosity as hostility, for instance — and gradually develop a distorted reality about the social world around them. That unconscious sense of threat can lead to an endless behavioral cycle in which a lonely person, in a mistaken attempt at self-protection, sends out signals of disinterest or even hostility, which then causes others to withdraw

"The consequences of isolation and loneliness are severe: negative health outcomes, higher health care costs and even death," said Senator Susan Collins (R-Maine), chairman of the Senate Special Committee on Aging, at a hearing in 2017. "Just as we did when we made a national commitment to cut smoking rates in this country," Collins went on, "we should explore approaches to reducing isolation and loneliness."

"Loneliness," Cacioppo observes, "is the discrepancy between what you want from your relationships and what you actually have."

What to do about it

One effective method may be cognitive behavioral therapy (CBT), which can help a lonely individual better understand how his or her assumptions and behavior might be working against the desire to connect with others. In England, Royal College of General Practitioners Chair Helen Stokes-Lampard recommends prescribing fewer pills and more "social prescribing," as in East Lancashire's "Green Dreams" program, where general practitioners (GPs) referred patients to voluntary work in outdoor gardens (see nature therapy in next section). This resulted in a 27 percent rise in reports of physical and mental health (and a 20 percent drop-in doctor appointments). She says successful schemes include walking groups, knitting groups and linking patients with local voluntary organizations, "which can really help to give people a sense of purpose."

A set of steps from WebMD:

Be kind to yourself

Your inner critic can feed feelings of loneliness. If you think you're different from other people or that you don't fit in, it can be harder to bond with others. You could get stuck in a loneliness rut. Recognize your thoughts and see them as a chance to make some changes.

"Loneliness is like pain," says David Cates, PhD, director of behavioral health at Nebraska Medicine in Omaha, NE. "It can be hard to measure, but you know when you feel it." Recognizing that you're out of sorts can be a sign that you may need more time with friends and family.

Be kind to others

Taking time out of your schedule to help others can be a great help. Lending a hand can unlock your inner joy and help you feel like part of a larger community. Check on an older relative or neighbor. Volunteer for a soup kitchen or for a virtual community event.

"We know people are hurting nationally because of the pandemic," Cates says. "The truth is we were dealing with loneliness and lack of social connections long before a global pandemic." Experts like Cates note the decline in social networks that can result from things like smaller family sizes, an increase in social media, families living farther apart, and having fewer bonds with volunteer and religious groups.

Plan ahead

There are days on the calendar that can make you sad. Plan ahead for tough days or seasons and put something fun on the calendar. Try to meet safely with friends or family. When a day (or time of year) you dread has something you're looking forward to instead, it can help.

"I call it proactive self-care," Hightower says. "Recognize that you expect to feel lonely during a certain time and be gentler with yourself." Plan a drive or to meet with friends. Looking forward to something joyful can bring joy.

Adopt a pet

If you have a fur baby already, you can likely share the benefits of having a pet at home. If not, consider welcoming one to your family. Research suggests having a pet can lower blood pressure, improve your mood, and ease stress. The extra cuddly company can also help if you're feeling lonely. Make sure you can handle the costs and extra tasks required, though.

Use social media wisely

Hopping onto social media can help you feel connected. But too much time online can lead to loneliness.

"Social media can sometimes trick your mind into thinking you're making real connections when you're not," Hightower says. "Social media isn't bad, but it shouldn't replace real connections."

Take a look at how much time you spend online. "We're so focused on likes, but those don't translate into feelings of connection," says Adam Brown, PhD, an associate professor of psychology at the New School for Social Research in New York City. Instead, use social media to help you make connections that go beyond likes and comments. Play online games with your family and friends. Try out apps that let you watch a show or movie with another person.

Rediscover a hobby

A hobby -- even one you do alone -- can help. That magical moment where you get lost in doing something you enjoy can push you past loneliness. You might hear it called "flow" or "being in the zone."

You could take up an old hobby like reading, cooking, photography, or yoga. Things that involve your hands (like knitting and painting) can also help you lose track of time -- in a good way. Or sign up to learn a new hobby. Try an online self-paced course or check out some online videos. You'll meet people with common interests along the way.

Reconnect with others

You don't need a cast of thousands to stop feeling lonely. Experts say that having a few close friends can make a big difference. Start with a phone call and then consider scheduling an online chat or a coffee or tea that you enjoy in person or virtually together.

Check in with others, knowing they may also find it hard to leave their comfort zone, too. Restart a family game night or plan a monthly online party with friends across the miles.

Find your why

Finding a sense of purpose may seem like a solo mission, but it isn't. Purpose is rooted in working with others. When you find your life's calling, you'll also often find those on the same path with you. Part of this may come from reconnecting to your faith or spending time reflecting.

Digging into your roots can also help define your purpose. Hearing stories about your family history can ease depression and boost self-esteem, Brown says. "Learning about how our family members have gotten through tough times can help us put our challenges in context."

Brown says research suggests nostalgic activities like flipping through old family photos can help you feel more connected.

Get outside

Whether you're with a friend or alone, Spending time in nature can raise your mood. "There is quite a bit of research that shows being out in nature can help people with loneliness," Brown says.

Take a scenic drive. Walk at the park alone or with a friend. Take a day off from work or family duties and enjoy a day at the beach, the lake, or a trail. If you work from home, set up your office outdoors when the weather is nice.

Move your body

Moving has a host of benefits, including helping you beat the blues of loneliness. Try dance, yoga, or going for a walk, or find an exercise class online. Staying active can help with depression, anxiety, stress, and a host of other things that can come with being lonely.

Don't have time or the energy for a long workout? No problem. Start with 5 to 10 minutes each day and build from there. Studies show moderate exercise -- where you breathe heavier than normal and get a little warm -- can have great benefits.

Seek therapy

Everyone feels lonesome from time to time. But experts say there's a problem if you feel:

- Lonely more than once a week
- Empty
- Like you don't belong

If you can't shake these feelings, you might need to talk to a counselor. The loss of a loved one, divorce, retirement, or moving to a new town can unleash lonely feelings. A therapist can help you work through these moments and give you tools to make them better.

Learn to cherish alone time

It may sound strange but spending time alone can help if you feel lonely. "It's important to distinguish between loneliness and social isolation," Cates says. Loneliness is subjective. There are people who are fairly isolated who aren't lonely and others who are around a lot of people with a deep sense of loneliness.

Spending time with yourself can help you feel recharged; bring greater clarity and focus, and boost creativity. It can also help you with your relationships, as spending quality time with yourself can help you appreciate your time with others. As with anything, balance is key. If you're spending too much time alone, your gut will tell you. You may feel something is off. That can be a good sign to get back in touch with others.

Loneliness doesn't have to be a constant in your life. Making a few changes can return the joy, connection, and friendships that are waiting around the corner.

Sixth Pillar:
Nature Therapy/Forest Bathing/eco-Therapy

Long before I heard the term nature therapy or forest-bathing, I cherished time among plants, trees, and the woods. I knew nothing about the science behind the benefits, only that it brought a calmness that I only experienced there.

The botanical gardens in both Singapore and Sydney are world-class. During my time living in both cities, I would either walk or do my daily run, through these gardens. The sensory experience, I could only describe as being a really good one. If pressed, I would mention the visual impact of all the blue sky, and variety of various trees. I had never heard the term *cortisol* (stress brain chemical) or *phyton* (plant/tree chemical), or how trees and all plants are imbued with *phyton* as a means of keeping tree and plant viruses at bay and how this same chemical lowers the cortisol level in the human brain.

In her inspiring work, *The Well-Gardened Mind,* Dr. Sue Stuart Smith, psychiatrist and psychotherapist in the United Kingdom credits the poet William Wordsworth with exploring more than anyone else on the influence of nature on the inner life of the mind. "He was psychologically prescient, and his ability to tune in to the subconscious means he is sometimes regarded as the forerunner of psychoanalytic thinking." He was a gardener, in addition to his day job of being perhaps England's greatest poet. He frequently worked on his poems in his garden. His parents had died when he and his sister were children. They cultivated vegetables, medicinal herbs and other useful plants.

"I turn to gardening as way of calming and decompressing my mind, Smith says. "Somehow, the jangle of competing thoughts inside my head clears and settles." The designer of New York's Central Park, Frederick Law Olmstead wrote, "Beautiful natural scenery, employs the mind without fatigue and yet it exercises it, enlivens it, and thus, through the influence of the mind over the body, gives the effect of refreshing rest and re-invigoration of the whole system." These words by Olmstead, written in the nineteenth century are orders of magnitude more applicable today, "city dwellers suffer from a range of afflictions, such as nervous tension, anxiety, hateful disposition, impatience and irritability." All acts of violence originate in an agitated mind, and the direct causal link between high crime rates in our cities and the conditions Olmstead wrote about are patently obvious

Forest therapy, or as it is known in Japan, *forest bathing* is an important, but little discussed technique for dealing with the stress and anxiety of life today. It may be hard to believe that there is somewhere more stressed and anxious than America, but Japan arguably is. It is a country with a "burnout" epidemic and a soaring suicide rate.

The New York based artist and designer M Daugherty says "It's a practice that very easy, but something that we've gotten away from as a society. We live in a go, go, go, go and doing more is revered as better. Forest therapy takes us out of that grind, in a nervous system that just constantly on edge, and brings us back into our senses." Studies out of Japan show that leisurely forest walks decrease cortisol levels, lower blood pressure, heart rate and reduce anxiety. Recognizing those benefits, in 1982, the Japanese Ministry of Agriculture, Forestry and Fisheries even coined a term for it: shinrin-yoku. It means taking in the forest atmosphere or "forest bathing," and the ministry encourages people to visit forests to relieve stress and improve health.

Forests, trees and health: Spending time outdoors and in forests makes us healthier:

Exposure to forests boosts our immune system. While we breathe in the fresh air, we breathe in phytoncides-- *phytons* for short. These airborne chemicals, natural to all plants are emitted into the air to protect themselves from insects. Phytons fight plant disease. When people breathe in these chemicals, as we hike through a forest, our bodies respond by increasing the number and activity of a type of white blood cell called natural killer cells or NK. These cells kill tumor- and virus-infected cells in our bodies. In one study, increased NK activity from a 3-day, 2-night forest bathing trip lasted for more than 30 days. Japanese researchers are currently exploring whether exposure to forests can help prevent certain kinds of cancer.

Time spent around trees and looking at trees reduces anxiety, and blood pressure and improves mood. Numerous studies show that both exercising in forests and simply sitting looking at trees reduce blood pressure as well as the stress-related hormones cortisol and adrenaline. These forest bathing trips, are shown to significantly decrease the scores for anxiety, depression, anger, confusion and fatigue. And because stress inhibits the immune system, the stress-reduction benefits of forests are further magnified.

Urban green spaces are just as important as rural forests. After what has been called the "great migration"—the movement from farms and rural areas following World War II, about 85% of the US population lives in suburban and urban areas and may not have access to traditional rural forests. Gardens, parks and street trees make up what is called an urban and community forest. These pockets of greenspace are vitally important in offsetting some of the negative impact of life in the concrete jungle, because they are the sources of our daily access to trees.

Spending time in nature helps you focus. Busy lives with jobs, school, and family life can mentally drain us. Spending time in nature, looking at plants, water, birds and other aspects of nature gives the cognitive portion of our brain a break, allowing us to focus better and renew our ability to be patient.

From the poet Wordsworth to one of America's greatest football coaches, Vince Dooley: Hall of Fame football coach and Master Gardener

American football, arguably the most brutal of sports and one of its most accomplished coaching icons, who has found peace and solitude in gardening and becoming a world-respected authority on its beauty and benefits to the mind and spirit

Excerpted from Garden and Gun

> "He spent his career as a football man. Twenty-five years as head coach at the University of Georgia, with 201 wins, six SEC titles, and one national championship (the 1980 team led by the great Herschel Walker). Twenty-four years as the Bulldogs' athletic director, a position he kept after retiring as coach in 1988. A member of the College Football Hall of Fame. To the surprise of everyone he knows—including himself—Vince Dooley has devoted his life to plants over the last twenty years, becoming a master gardener along the way. (That's an official title, in fact, bestowed by the UGA Cooperative Extension office.) Now, at eighty-four, he travels the world visiting gardens and speaking at gardening conferences. He has written a book, *Vince Dooley's Garden*. He has a camellia *and* hydrangea named after him.

AWE Walks

One effective way to deal with social disconnection, anxiety, and sadness is "awe"—that emotional reaction we have when in the presence of vast things of great majesty like the night sky on a clear night, a walk in the woods and particularly some of our most majestic national parks and landmarks.

Sixty participants in a recent study from the American Psychological Association took weekly 15-minute outdoor walks for 8 weeks. The participants were randomly assigned to an awe walk group, which oriented them to experience awe during their walks, or to a control walk group. Participants took photographs of themselves during each walk and rated their emotional experience. Each day, they reported on their daily emotional experience outside of the walk context. Participants also completed pre-and postintervention measures of anxiety, depression, and life satisfaction. Compared with participants who took control walks, those who took awe walks experienced greater awe during their walks and exhibited an increasingly "small self" in their photographs over time. They reported greater joy and positive emotions during their walks, and greater decreases in daily distress.

I have travelled to 65 countries across the globe, many on business and others for pleasure. The most awe-inspiring have been those with the bluest sky, mountains is some cases, vast expanses of water: The Milford Track (New Zealand), Mount Everest (my son and I reached the base camp), the Maldives (endless white sands and blue water), Patagonia in Chile (endless rolling hills and mountains), Yellowstone and Glacier National Parks, Krueger National Park (South Africa), Great Barrier Reef (scuba diving in Australia) et al.

What to do about it

Bucket (faith, hugs, dogs, laughter, cold showers, sighing see pg 79 of Burnout book, knitting (see notes)

YOUR 66 DAY LIFE-CHANGING REGIMEN

CHAPTER SEVEN

*"I no longer fear storms, for I am now
learning how to sail my ship"*
Louisa May Alcott

The seas of life are choppy. We can't change the external events in our lives, but we can adopt methods and techniques to navigate the choppy seas and even the periodic tsunamis that can otherwise traumatize.

Sixty-Six Days:

Regimens for improving our self-care often become round trips. We often lack the personal discipline to execute with the commitment necessary to install the change a permanent new mode of behavior in our life. The round trip from the old behavior to the new, more healthy, age-defying, one too often lasts for a short time until we decided its too hard, or we "don't have time". Think back on the times new years resolutions haven't made it to the end of January. Research now discredits the earlier formula of twenty-one days. The highly respected University College of London study has firmly established that it takes more than two months, hence the sixty-six day formula. A dedicated ccommitment to the Six Pillars Regimen provided here will truly change your life. Go forward and execute with discipline.

DO IT

"Without execution, vision is just another word for hallucination"

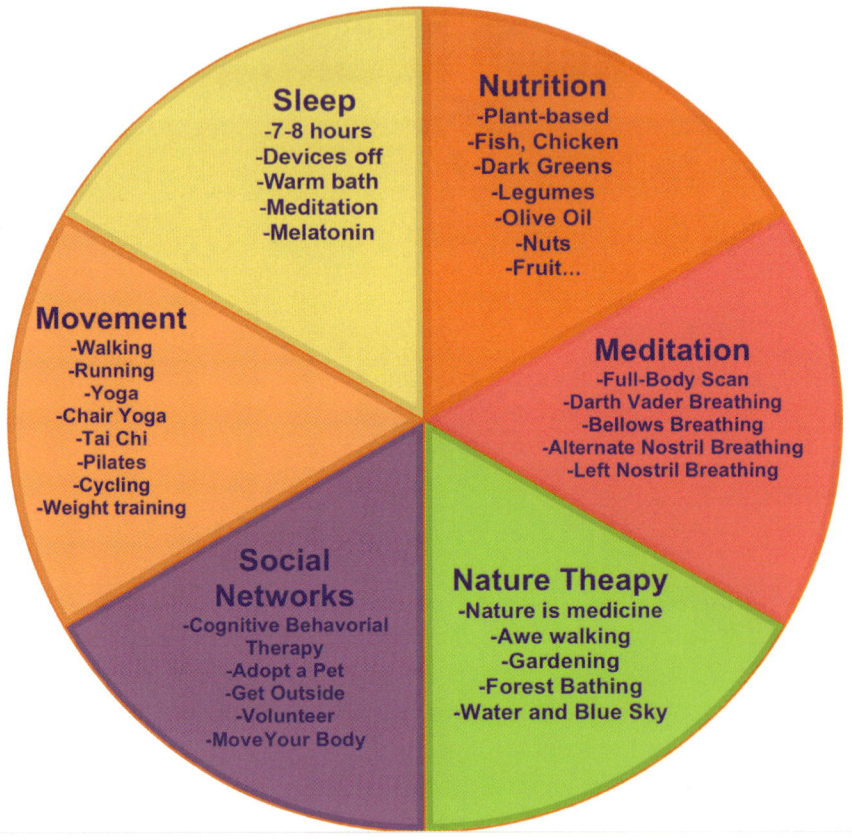

SIX PILLARS OF WELL-BEING
MANAGE YOUR MIND / MANAGE YOUR LIFE

Sleep
-7-8 hours
-Devices off
-Warm bath
-Meditation
-Melatonin

Nutrition
-Plant-based
-Fish, Chicken
-Dark Greens
-Legumes
-Olive Oil
-Nuts
-Fruit...

Movement
-Walking
-Running
-Yoga
-Chair Yoga
-Tai Chi
-Pilates
-Cycling
-Weight training

Meditation
-Full-Body Scan
-Darth Vader Breathing
-Bellows Breathing
-Alternate Nostril Breathing
-Left Nostril Breathing

Social Networks
-Cognitive Behavorial Therapy
-Adopt a Pet
-Get Outside
-Volunteer
-Move Your Body

Nature Theapy
-Nature is medicine
-Awe walking
-Gardening
-Forest Bathing
-Water and Blue Sky

MIND FITNESS
Your 66 Day Regimen

Exiting the A.S.A.P. Lane!

6 PILLARS
Sleep

Meditation

Movement

Nutrition

Social Network

Grounding

EXCUSES
I'm not flexible enough

It's too hard

My body type not right

My church is opposed

It's not real exercise

Can't do the poses

I'm too old

I'm too busy

I'm in a wheelchair

I'm too far gone

10 COMMANDMENTS OF WELL-BEING
If you can breathe, you can do this

Mindful breathing is the Yellow Brick Road

Manage stress one breath at a time

The time is always just NOW

Make time for health now, or be forced to make time for illness later

Fitness is body, mind and spirit, not just physical

Commit to consistent practice; the monkey never rests

Go to your limit, never past it

First, a calm mind, then strength, flexibility and balance

You are not your age

SLEEP:
7-8 HOURS

NAPS

Sleep deprivation is a killer!

NUTRITION:
3-5 serving of fruits and vegetables per day

Healthy Protein

Healthy fats; nuts, avocados

Eat a balanced diet

MOVEMENT:
Yoga

Running

Walking

Cycling

Stimulate the Vagus Nerve

SOCIAL NETWORK:
Cultivate friends and family

Studying and working in public space

Get rid of toxic relationships

GROUNDING:
Exposure to nature

Mindful walking

Barefoot on grass

Connect with the earth

MEDITATION:
(see apps section below)

Darth Vader Breath

Taco Method

Alternate Nostril Method

Bellows Breath Methos

I-Rest Method

Sedate the Monkey!

APPS:
Meditation: *Insight Timer, Calm, HeadSpace*

Yoga: *FitStar Yoga, Down Dog, 19 Minute Yoga*